Models of Adult Religious Education Practice

Models of Adult Religious Education Practice

R.E.Y. Wickett

Religious Education Press
Birmingham, Alabama

Library of Congress Cataloging-in-Publication Data

Wickett, R. E. Y.
    Models of adult religious education practice / R.E.Y. Wickett.
    Includes bibliographical references and index.
    ISBN 0-89135-083-7
    1. Religious education of adults.   I. Title.
  BL42.W53   1991   91-38071
  268'.434—dc20   CIP

Religious Education Press, Inc.
5316 Meadow Brook Road
Birmingham, Alabama 35242
10 9 8 7 6 5 4 3 2

Religious Education Press publishes books exclusively in religious education
and in areas closely related to religious education. It is committed to enhanc-
ing and professionalizing religious education through the publication of
serious, significant, and scholarly works.

PUBLISHER TO THE PROFESSION

Prologue

This book is intended to provide a sound theoretical and practical introduction to adult religious education. It contains both traditional and alternative
approaches to practice. The general theoretical framework is provided in
the initial chapters, while the other chapters attempt to combine a specific theoretical base with suggestions for the implementation of each model.

Models provide us with a way to understand the complexities of practice. A framework is provided within which the practitioner can achieve a
sense of direction and, hopefully, some confidence. The models which are
described in this volume represent the major models with potential for application in adult religious education.

I make no apologies for the fact that I have deliberately excluded certain
models which I believe, rightly or wrongly, have no place in adult religious
education as I conceptualize this field. Competency-Based Education and
other models which resemble it are examples of models which may have a
place elsewhere, but there is no place for them in this volume.

What I have included are those models which I deem to be appropriate and
adaptable to the setting of adult religious education by their very nature and
the nature of adult religious education as I see it. The resulting models
include those which support individualized learning, individual learning in
group settings, and collective learning.

The models presented in this volume are either "adapted" from other settings or presented with my own particular perspective. Should you wish to
learn more about the original models and their workings, you will be able to
follow suggestions for future readings from any original source.

Adaptations were necessary in many circumstances because of the particular nature of adult religious education. I have attempted to be fair with the
original models while relating them specifically to the adult religious education context. The errors or misinterpretations must be attributed to this
author rather than the originators of the models.

It is clear that I owe a debt to several people for the inspiration and assistance which they provided during the processes of development and writing
of this book. Dean Murray Scharf of the College of Education and Principal
"Rusty" Brown of the College of Emmanuel and St. Chad at the University
of Saskatchewan provided critical support in the early stages and throughout
the process. Roland Wood gave both needed encouragement and financial
assistance at important moments. Peter Slater of the Faculty of Divinity at
Trinity College, Toronto, allocated a space to work and library access for a

period of time. My colleagues at the Ontario Institute for Studies in Education including Don Brundage, Lynn Davies, and Virginia Griffin were most helpful in various ways to the creative process. Allen Tough deserves special mention for his support at an important time in the process and throughout my career.

A special word of thanks is due to Carol Schick, a graduate student whose imagination and skill contributed to my thinking about practice in recent years. Her writing of an initial draft of chapter 4, which remains the essence of that chapter, and the preparation of the "covenants" assisted me to complete the work on schedule. I consider this chapter on the philosophical issues to be most important.

To the members of my family and friends who supported me during the difficult parts of the process, I wish to say a special thank you. It was nice to know that you were there.

R.E.Y. WICKETT

Contents

Part B

THE TRADITIONAL MODELS

Part C

ALTERNATIVE MODELS: THE INDIVIDUAL LEARNER

gious education activities? This chapter reviews the issues raised by research and the related literature from adult education and religious education which suggest the value of the search for alternate effective methods. The case for the support of individual learners and for the utilization of new approaches to group learning is considered.

The independent learner is discussed as a common member of religious communities and society as a whole. It may be necessary for this person to contact a resource person such as a church librarian or other adult religious educator from time to time. Suggested responses to this person's learning process are outlined in this chapter.

The nondirective tutorial, a one-to-one approach as described by C.O. Houle and with a considerable base in the educational philosophy of Carl Rogers, is presented in this chapter.

The learning covenant for one-to-one and group situations is reviewed in this chapter. This model is adapted from the model as presented by Malcolm Knowles. The basic assumptions and elements of the learning contract are presented.

Part D

ALTERNATIVE MODELS: THE INDIVIDUAL'S LEARNING IN GROUPS

Allen Tough has developed a model for the facilitation of learning based on a view of the classroom or group learning activity as merely the "tip of the iceberg" of total learning activity. This group model combines traditional adult education skills with a recognition of the broader context of learning.

Virginia Griffin's model provides a base for learning within a group. This model features a means by which the learner is encouraged to become more self-directed in the security of the group.

Part E

ALTERNATIVE MODELS: THE COMMUNITY MODELS OF LEARNING

Part F

DISTANCE EDUCATION: A NEW MODEL FOR A SPECIAL SITUATION

Part G

Chapter 1

Introduction

I must confess to you in the first part of this book that I am tempted to view adult religious educators as a type of "sub-species." There is no pejorative intention to this statement. It is simply meant to indicate that we fit somehow into larger groups of people who constitute a more readily identifiable segment of society. For some of us, this group will be known as religious educators; for others, it will be the group known as adult educators. Yet I am unable to resist the temptation to suggest that there is a clear need for our "sub-species" to continue to emerge in its own right.

What does it mean to be a "sub-species"? Clearly it means that historically the status which comes with being a fully recognized association of people with a defined sphere of activity has not come to us. The disadvantages of this situation range from a lack of status (which should not be a concern) to being a small portion of the budget (which should!).

The advantages of being a sub-species include our ability to draw upon the quite considerable resources of our larger constituencies in order to enhance our practice. This need not be a disadvantage as we can continue to relate to our colleagues from the other areas.

Another way of describing the existence of the adult religious educator is to see its derivation in the meeting of the two disciplines of adult education and religious education. Perhaps our group would be much enhanced if we were a true offspring of a full marriage between these two "species." Whatever the analogy is and however we choose to explore it, the need for the maturation of adult religious education will face us still.

Adult religious education is clearly in the process of coming of age. Some people have been slower than others to recognize the emergence of this vital area of ministry, but it has been emerging nevertheless. To confirm this, all we need to do is to look at the pews in our meeting places, at our communities, and at the findings of research on adult learning.

The responsibility for this emerging area is quite simply ours as adult religious educators to accept. We must move from the shadows of our former, larger groups. The importance of what we do is inescapable for those who see the relationship of learning to adult growth and development.

This book is written for the adult religious educator, or the member of the "sub-species," if you prefer. The person who should receive the most benefit from its pages will be the "thoughtful practitioner." This book was written with that particular type of person in mind. We have all met the person who likes to do things well and who believes that the quality of performance is based upon an understanding of the theoretical underpinnings of practice.

The theoretician may examine this book for its statements of theory and the practitioner may search for "handy" advice. I hope that both will find something of interest in its pages. It is my belief, however, that the person who will gain the most has elements of both theory and practice in mind as the pages are turned.

If we are to be successful in fulfilling our responsibilities in the context of adult religious education we shall need to identify our field of activity and its strengths and weaknesses. We must draw both knowledge and skill from the other members of the two major groups of which we have been sub-groups. This book is concerned with part of that latter activity. It will review various aspects of adult education with particular attention to the models which operate currently in the field. This will be done with the intention to assist adult religious educators to benefit from those things which have been learned by our colleagues in adult education.

As an adult educator who has been involved in adult religious education as a theoretician, practitioner, and researcher, I shall attempt to review certain key aspects of adult education practice for the reader. We can learn from the work of our adult education colleagues if we proceed in appropriate ways. What I mean by this is that we can learn from adult education through both examination and adaptation.

I do not expect everything done in the broad field of adult education to be relevant or workable in the specific field of adult religious education. Some aspects of adult religious education have very specific requirements. To put it simply, our institutions, our learners, and our content areas frequently have their own specific requirements which are different from those of secular agencies and content areas. What we must do is to adapt, where appropriate, the models of adult education to suit our situations in adult religious education.

This book represents a sincere attempt to adapt the important models which are utilized in the field of adult education for use by the adult religious educator and to describe briefly their underlying foundations in research and philosophy. These models will be described in a manner that is related to the particular requirements of adult religious education.

Where the models have been used extensively in a religious context, the lessons will be drawn more easily. Some evaluation of these more frequently used models will be made as their strengths and weaknesses are described in each section or chapter. Where the models have not been used extensively in adult religious education, more care will be taken to insure that the adaptation to the adult religious education context is carried out appropriately.

MODELS OF TEACHING AND LEARNING

It would be helpful to the reader to have some idea of the nature of a model. This next section will explore the meaning I shall ascribe to the word in the context of this work. The definition of an educational model takes on specific manifestations which make it different from other types of models in fields such as politics, economics, and sociology.

The features of a model of teaching must have implications for the planning process as well as the actual delivery of content. The classic volume on educational models is the popular book by Bruce Joyce and Marsha Weil, entitled *Models of Teaching*. This book describes a model as "a plan or pattern that we can use to design face-to-face teaching in classrooms or tutorial settings and to shape instructional materials—including books, films, tapes, and computer-mediated programs and curricula (long-term courses of study). Each model guides us as we design instruction to help students achieve various objectives."[1]

As valuable as the definition by Joyce and Weil may be to some educators, I wish to move beyond it for the field of adult religious education. The difficulty I have with this approach to educational models is in its emphasis on the planning and teaching, as directed by the educator, to assist the learner to achieve an identified objective. If we expand our concept to "learning" and incorporate the characteristics of adulthood, we shall need to move beyond the limitations of this definition of a model.

I propose the following definition of a new educational model in order to allow the learner to be involved in a fashion which goes beyond the narrower limits. "A model will assist the educator to understand the nature of the learner's situation and to create a context in which the learner will be enabled to learn and grow through an appropriate process." The focus in my definition of an educational model is clearly on the learner while the educator is defined in relation to the learner. The learner is also important to Joyce and Weil, but the issue is one of emphasis rather than lack of importance.

This approach clearly presupposes the need to be practical and interactive with the learner. Successful learning is a goal common to both types of models, but the model of Joyce and Weil holds the goal and objective as clear and precise. In religious growth and development we may find it difficult to give precise definitions to goals and objectives at the start of the process.

An educational model provides a framework for the practice of education. It should contain the important elements which will ensure an appropriate teaching/learning interaction leading to a successful learning outcome. Educators should be able to examine it critically in order to determine its potential for success. I believe that a model should be described in a manner which enables the practitioner to pursue it successfully.

Educational models frequently derive from the activities of innovative, thoughtful practitioners. A successful practitioner who wants to do everything possible to enable learning will seek to improve on existing options. Many such practitioners benefit from the dynamics of the teaching/learning situation.

The influence of theory should not be denied when one considers the derivation of models. It is the thoughtful, well-read practitioner who will have an excellent opportunity to try to implement the suggestions which come from theoretical writings.

In the final analysis, an effective educational model represents the merging of carefully developed theory and successful practice. The refinement of practice through this type of merger should apply equally to old and new models of education.

The model should provide a framework for decision making and other process-related activities. It must assist the practitioner to know what is to be done when as well as how it is to be done and in what circumstances it should be done. When the presentation of a model is complete, the practitioner should have some confidence in the model and his or her abilities to proceed with some hope of success.

Some models presented in this book have their origins in the research and writing of Malcolm Knowles[2] concerning the traditional approach and of Allen Tough,[3] C.O. Houle,[4] and Malcolm Knowles[5] about self-directed learning. Other models find their inspiration in the social action orientation as seen in the work of authors like Paulo Freire.[6] The book is not limited solely to models which originate in North America, but it will appear in the final analysis of the chapters that these models predominate. Perhaps that is because the models which are most prevalent in North America have already found their way into our collective thinking.

Please note that the models which are presented are inspired by the existing models of adult education but not without proposed adaptation to the content and context of adult religious education. Any weaknesses which are found are likely to be derived from the attempt to adapt rather than the use of the original models as presented by the various authors in their own writings.

A significant part of the book will review the traditional model of adult education based on the now traditional, andragogical approach of Malcolm

Knowles. This fine author and practitioner rightly deserves a place of honor in our hearts for his commitment to adult education in general as well as to adult religious education. The principles of andragogy have guided the practice of the vast majority of adult education practitioners for more than two decades.

Malcolm Knowles has been influenced, along with many other authors, researchers, and practitioners, by the research and writing of Allen Tough. The change in the thinking of adult educators from the "course" as the focus to learning and the activities of the individual learner truly began with Allen Tough and his colleague and professor at the University of Chicago, C.O. Houle. Tough's work and the work of other colleagues in the self-direction of learning have given us a fresh approach to the learning process.

Paulo Freire has forced all educators who read his work to consider the social implications of their actions. As people with values and beliefs which involve religious communities, we must examine the implications of these ideas for their messages to our communities.

Freire's participation in the work of the World Council of Churches in Geneva for a number of years involved adult religious education. His travels and work during this period are less well known than his famous work in adult literacy, but we can still learn much from his theory and practice.

No author should suggest that a method or model which has been developed in one setting should automatically be advocated for use in other settings. None of the previously mentioned authors would wish models to be used indiscriminately. I believe they have shared their experiences and the theoretical aspects of their work, but they ask others to consider the implications of what they have written.

What I have attempted to do in this book is to describe certain models for adult religious education based upon their adult education counterparts. I do not advocate the use of all adult education models or methods for use in the context of religious education for adults. The ones I do advocate are models which are, in my opinion, useful and provide effective options for the practitioner who is prepared to engage thoughtfully in work with learners.

A significant approach to the categorization of "educational situations" is found in C.O. Houle's book, *The Design of Education*.[7] The categories range from "independent study" to the "mass" educational situation. This book will comment directly upon those particular categories which I feel are most useful to the practitioner of adult religious education. Certain categories will be subsumed under the traditional model of adult education based upon M.S. Knowles' andragogical principles. Other models have been included in the section of the book on alternative models.

Houle's categories include independent study, one-to-one educational situations, and various forms of educational situations with a variety of groups. Our involvement in independent study is extremely limited by its very nature. The one-to-one situation provides a very fruitful arena for discussion because of the special needs within the context of adult religious education. Adult religious educators have seen the group situation as the most viable context for activity for many years although the form and nature of the enterprise has varied considerably.

The following list of Houle's categories includes both the categories utilized in this book and others which may be worthy of future consideration:

1. Independent Study
2. Tutorial Teaching
3. Learning Group
4. Teacher-Directed Group Instruction
5. Committee-Guided Group Learning
6. Collaborative Group Education
7. Creating an Educational Institution
8. Designing a New Institutional Format
9. Designing New Activities in Established Formats
10. Collaborative Institutional Planning
11. Mass Education[8]

Houle's system considers the particular nature of the educational activity, the institutional (or noninstitutional) context, planning and evaluation, and the life context of the learning.

Houle provides us with the theoretical framework which enables a systematic approach to the field. This may be contrasted with the quite practical approach of Malcolm Knowles. Jerold Apps has built upon the legacy of both of these earlier authors[9] and related the practical aspects of program development to the religious education of adults.[10]

WHY ADULT RELIGIOUS EDUCATION?

This critical question needs to be answered before the adult religious educator proceeds to work with learners. The answer will be found in more than one dimension. There will be both individual and communal answers which need to be considered. The individual answer will lie in relation to both the educator and the learner. The communal answer will involve the institution and the faith community, however defined, in which it exists.

To be effective, the adult religious educator should consider and determine some form of an answer to these questions. Individual educators should be able to articulate clearly their own reasons. They should strive also to have the institution or faith community articulate its reasons wherever applicable.

Perhaps the simple phrases "to know" and "to grow" can be applied to help us to answer our question. Adult religious education is an enabler of these two processes in relation to the religious context. These phrases may be used in relation to both adults and children so they yield something which is not unique to adult religious education.

Leon McKenzie refers to the continuum of life and its relationship to adult religious education through the separation of adult education from child education by the application of Knowles' theory of andragogy.[11] Life is indeed a continuum, but we can identify the parts thereof. The phrases "to know" and "to grow" may have different meanings in different parts of the life continuum.

Knowledge inevitably leads to the process of change, in my opinion, and it may be difficult to separate our two phrases easily. Perhaps we need to consider the phrases from the perspective of the educator who can see them more readily as goals for his or her activities. It would be easier to identify goals and objectives through the utilization of one phrase or the other in order to define our educational direction.

The learner, on the other hand, may not separate and identify his goals as precisely. It is my observation that many learners do not identify their goals and objectives with the same precision as the educator who focuses on behavioral objectives nor do they supply a plan for a group's or individual's learning program which is as specific as the educator's plan.

The real purpose of adult religious education should be integrated with the purpose of religion. We cannot separate the educational component from the broader purpose which it serves. This means that those who seek knowledge or growth will do so in a context of a religion and frequently within a faith community and its institutions.

I believe that Leon McKenzie and James Fowler have identified the critical component through their writings on adult religious education and faith development respectively. They both describe *meaning* as the critical component of the definition of these two interrelated areas. This "meaning" to which they refer is the greater meaning which gives definition to all of our being.

McKenzie has presented this concept as the basis for adult religious education in two well-written pieces. The first may be found in his own book, *The Religious Education of Adults*, and the second is a chapter which forms the introduction to Nancy Foltz's book, *Handbook of Adult Religious Education*.[12] His diagrammatic presentation on the centrality of meaning, as shown in Figure 1, provides a simple but powerful framework for our work as adult religious educators.

Figure 1[13]

"Meaning" and adult religious education

Service

Fowler describes faith as "an orientation of the total person, giving purpose and goals to one's hopes and striving, thoughts and actions."[14] The very essence of being is found in the faith aspect of the human being for this author. It is the essential search for this "quest for meaning" that fuels our individual, developmental journey.

It may be helpful to see the "quest for meaning" as a form of journey. We can thus begin to examine different aspects of the journey and the different perspectives which people have of it along the way.

There are different parts to this journey according to Fowler. He has divided it up into what he calls stages during which the nature of the faith journey can be described in different ways. It is important to remember that the journey is one of growth and change, of a progressive process whereby we come closer to the fullness of meaning for ourselves.

It is possible to identify stages or phases during this journey when specific characteristics of the stage may be described. These characteristics are different from those of earlier or later stages, although they are not unrelated. The relationship may be found in the way each period is built upon its predecessors. This guarantees the need for a sequence of discernible periods.

THE CONTEXT OF ADULT RELIGIOUS EDUCATION

The context of adult religious education and learning should be understood before one proceeds with the implementation of programs. A church, synagogue, or any other institution must develop policies which enable the learning to occur. These policies will be developed within the prevailing atmosphere and confines of the institution.

A policy will allow clerical and lay persons who are charged with implementation to proceed in some security and with some financial support for their activities. When the limits have been set carefully, a higher degree of success for learners and educators alike is more probable.

Please note that I do not see the educational component of the system as separate and distinct from the other facets of the institution or faith community's life. All education occurs within an environment which will have influence either implicitly or explicitly. One must recognize this influence and, where possible, give it the most positive shape.

If learning occurs through experience, the total experience of the faith community will be a factor. Educational programs can not exist at cross purposes with the environment. Liturgy and other aspects of the life of the community must be seen also as influential in relation to total learning.

THE SPECIAL NATURE OF ADULT RELIGIOUS EDUCATION

Perhaps the most critical aspect of adult religious education for all who would engage in this activity as learners or facilitators is that there is always an additional party to the process. This party is not seen nor are we always able to detect the "Presence." Yet our theology makes us aware of the reality of this "Presence" which many of us refer to as God.

If we know God in other parts of our life, how can we deny the presence of God in this aspect? It is not possible to deny this partner in our search for growth and change. John Hull, a British Christian educator, describes this learning partnership as involving Jesus Christ, God, and humanity[15] in the Christian context. Even those who have not found this conclusion will need to consider the Presence which appears to accompany us on the journey.

This path of learning involves a journey like no other we have ever taken because it is central to our being. No other learning has the same potential impact on all areas of our life. No other form of learning is quite so full of meaning because meaning is the focus.

Notes

1. Bruce Joyce and Marsha Weil, *Models of Teaching*, 3rd ed. (Englewood Cliffs, N.J.: Prentice-Hall, 1986), p.2.

2. Malcolm S. Knowles, *The Modern Practice of Adult Education: From Pedagogy to Andragogy*, Revised and Updated (Chicago: Follett, 1980).

3. Allen Tough, *The Adult's Learning Projects: A Fresh Approach to Theory and Practice in Adult Learning*, 2nd ed. (Toronto: The Ontario Institute for Studies in Education, 1979).

4. Cyril O. Houle, *The Design of Education* (San Francisco: Jossey-Bass, 1972)

5. See Malcolm S. Knowles, *Self-Directed Learning: A Guide for Learners and Teachers* (Chicago: Follett, 1975) and Malcolm S. Knowles, *Using Learning Contracts: Practical Approaches to Individualizing and Structuring Learning* (San Francisco: Jossey-Bass, 1986).

6. Paulo Freire, *Pedagogy of the Oppressed* (New York: Seabury, 1970).

7. Houle, *The Design of Education*, pp. 90-130.

8. Ibid., pp. 91-128.

9. J.W. Apps, *Improving Practice in Continuing Education* (San Francisco: Jossey-Bass, 1985).

10. J.W. Apps, *How to Improve Adult Education in Your Church* (Minneapolis: Augsburg, 1972).

11. Leon McKenzie, *The Religious Education of Adults* (Birmingham, Ala.: Religious Education Press, 1982), pp. 119-125.

12. See Leon McKenzie, "The Purposes and Scope of Adult Religious Education," in *Handbook of Adult Religious Education*, ed. Nancy T. Foltz (Birmingham, Ala.: Religious Education Press, 1986) and Leon McKenzie, *The Religious Education of Adults* (Birmingham, Ala.: Religious Education Press, 1982), pp. 126-127.

13. McKenzie, *The Religious Education of Adults*, p. 127.

14. James W. Fowler, *Stages of Faith: The Psychology of Human Development and the Quest for Meaning* (San Francisco: Harper & Row, 1981), p. 14.

15. John M. Hull, *What Prevents Christian Adults from Learning?* (London: SCM Press, 1985), chapter 5.

Chapter 2

The Adult Learner
and Religious Education

Who are the adult learners that will be involved in the process of religious education? What type of potential exists for adults to be involved in adult religious education? This chapter is concerned with an examination of the issue, "Who will be our learners and what will they learn?"

Initially, we should consider the fact that more adults have participated in adult education activities in recent times than prior records show. Patricia Cross refers to this in terms of the growth of the "learning society."[1] The reasons she cites for this include demographic change,[2] social change,[3] and technological change.[4] Within the particular changes within society, she cites such issues as rising educational attainment, changing career patterns, changing role of women, equal opportunity, and increased leisure time.[5]

In fact, our learners will represent the broad range of participants in the religious community and possibly others from the fringe or beyond the immediate faith community. The latter will be dependent on the nature of the broader community and the extent to which the faith community is open to others. The nature of the content will be a factor, of course, in the decisions about the involvement of others.

We must recognize that many groups will experience an incredible diversity among the membership of the faith community or the broader community which the faith community wishes to serve. There will be very sophisticated persons with high levels of knowledge and learning skills as well as those with other useful knowledge and skill levels. The group which must not be forgotten is the group that lacks these particular levels of knowledge and skill for learning. Opportunities must not be denied to these persons neither collectively nor individually.

11

It is a normal part of the process of adult development to continue to grow and change as a person. We can assume that virtually all adults will examine the critical issues of their faith, beliefs, attitudes, and values at some time during the adult years. Psychologists predict that this will happen, although there is no universal agreement as to when this examination will occur. If this is true, we can expect most adults to be potential participants in learning activities related to this normal developmental process.

We can assume that those who participate presently in our programs should continue to be involved. These people should be accommodated in any new ventures which proceed from our new activities. We may choose to offer a variety of models in our total religious education program in order to accommodate all parties. This will ensure the involvement of those who prefer certain models to the exclusion of others. Numbers and budget will be a factor in the decision to offer a broad range of learning activities.

New participants will be attracted by flexibility and the feeling that their learning will be supported to a successful conclusion. The barriers need to be taken down for this new group. Whether they are barriers of distance, time, accessibility, or feelings, we need to ensure that they are removed.

There is the potential for working with adults throughout the adult years. In her volume, *Handbook of Adult Religious Education*,[6] Nancy Foltz has included chapters with reference to the process of working with each different age group during adulthood in the chapters on young,[7] middle,[8] and older[9] adults. There are no insurmountable barriers to the participation of all age groups if we choose to remove those barriers which we have often created. It should also be noted that it is possible to have adult education activities in concert with each age group including those who have not yet achieved adulthood. James White has described "intergenerational" programing in his book on the subject.[10] This model for programing will be examined in one of the chapters of this book.

There are those persons with specific needs who will wish to learn in order to cope with life situations involving relationships such as marriage, parenting, and divorce. Others will face specific problems such as illness or death. There will be an immediacy to these situations to which we must be prepared to respond.

Our faith communities have not always responded adequately to special groups such as racial minorities, the disadvantaged, or handicapped persons in the most appropriate ways. If we can now build ramps and organize special ministries, we should consider the educational programs which will make these persons an important part of our community's life.

The "skills" to which I refer in the context of adult religious education are not normally the physical skills to be learned in other educational contexts. I am concerned more with the application of social skills which are used for ministry or for personal growth.

Learners will be interested in acquiring these skills for various reasons. This group can be divided into those who require skills for their own personal development and those who require skills for ministry in order to serve. Both skill areas need to be accommodated in our programs.

Skills for personal use will include the skills that enable growth and the skills of self-education which enable both the self-directed learner and the self-directed group. Skills for growth will range from the skills of prayer and meditation to skills for self-analysis and examination. I hardly need to suggest the interconnectedness of these areas. Learners may, however, portray them in various ways.

The skills of the self-directed learner are intended to enable the learner to take responsibility for the overall process of learning. The learner may look to the facilitator to provide the requisite background to develop these skills.

The need for skills which enable the group to become self-directed is to be found among learners who wish to achieve common, community-related goals. This group of learners wants to work together and will benefit from gaining the skills which will make this possible.

SKILLS FOR MINISTRY

The importance of lay ministry, whether paid or voluntary, has been recognized for many years in certain religious groups while others have begun more recently to recognize the value of a core group of competent, trained lay ministers to assist the faith community to achieve its goals. Ministry can be effective if individuals have the requisite skills to perform the associated tasks.

The duly trained and ordained ministry also requires constant renewal in order to remain effective. Many models described in this volume can be utilized effectively with this group as well as with the laity.

It is reasonable to suggest that more specialization is required for those who are more highly trained at the start. An individual with skills in a secular occupation may be able to make use of those skills in a church context with minimal training. A social worker who wishes to visit the sick or an accountant who will keep the church books are good examples of skilled lay persons.

Many models do provide an adequate basis for training for skills in ministry. It is critical that the model chosen identify clearly the level of skills of the individual and the precise skills required for the activity involved. Only through a comparison of the two skill levels can we identify the need for learning. Individualization through the models of contracting and one-to-one tutoring may be one solution to the problem of new skills for those of quite distinct needs and skill levels.

Learners may need to relearn previously forgotten skills or unlearn skills which involve a different application than is required for a form of ministry.

There is a need, in many instances, to integrate the skills which a learner has with the new skills which will be required for future ministry.

LEARNING FOR PERSONAL GROWTH

The evidence that learners are strongly motivated to grow and change at various points in their lives is overwhelming. Learners will have periods when the search for knowledge and understanding is critical to growth. The issue for adult religious educators involves the manner in which learners will respond to these feelings.

The learner will often identify the need within himself or herself in order to proceed. The precise nature of the need does not have to be clear. In many instances, we can see that the search is as important to the clarification of the need as the original identification of it. People may sense a mere feeling of need to begin the search for growth. Learners, in what has been labeled by Daniel Levinson[11] as a "transitional stage," will work on the transition without a full understanding of its implications.

It may be critical to assist these learners to identify as clearly as possible where they wish to proceed to grow and change. This may be done in the early stages of the learning process, but learners who have no sense beyond a malaise will have difficulty in obtaining a sense of direction.

These learners will potentially come from diverse social groups. Each person is faced with the need to learn in the context of a changing self and a changing environment. What we believe to be true about our own self and our world will not continue to be true necessarily throughout the normal life span. One needs only to consider the aging process and the way our communities have changed in recent history to know the truth of this statement.

LEARNING FOR SOCIAL CHANGE

There are moments when adults perceive the difference between the world as it should or could be and the world as it is. Many learners will choose to learn in order to affect change in the world as they know it. These learners will frequently come together because the group will be able to accomplish more than any individual within the social context.

The religious context of this type of learning should not be discounted. Most religions consider that human behavior ought to reflect certain higher ideals. These ideals can be accomplished at times in a better social context, therefore social change becomes an imperative.

The impact of this form of learning on the faith community may be quite dramatic. The process of changing society may involve changes in the faith community which are exhilarating to some but threatening to others. As the faith community is a human institution, it will not be immune to the need to change and grow to be consistent with the needs of its members and the society of which they are a part. The key will be to insure that it does not compromise its basic beliefs but attempts to live out these beliefs in the community context.

Learners who are committed to the higher ideals of a religion may strive to support religious groups to effect change in the broader world. They will learn more about these higher ideals as well as the implementation of social change in the process.

LEARNING FOR SOCIAL REASONS

There is a group of learners who indicate that they participate in learning activities because of the relationships with others that result from the learning activity. Allen Tough describes the reasons provided by this type of learner in his book, *Why Adults Learn.*[12] It is possible to impute from these reasons certain characteristics of learners.

Tough describes one reason why adults learn as related to the fact that "others notice."[13] We know that learners may attend courses in order to please others, as is the case with the employee who takes a job-related course in order to impress his or her employer. It may be the situation for some learners that they wish someone who is involved in the course to take notice.

It would appear to me that these reasons are valid to the individuals who participate in the course and that they are normally combined, according to Tough, with other reasons.[14] These other reasons may be as important or more important that the social reasons. These other reasons may be the reasons why a particular class was chosen.

The responsibility of the facilitator is to recognize these reasons and to accept them. A positive adult learning experience in a group will involve group interaction and appropriate recognition of any accomplishments for members.

LEARNING FOR THE SAKE OF LEARNING

Stephen Brookfield makes reference to learning which is meaningful to adults with no specific goal in mind.[15] Some learners engage in learning which brings joy and meaning in and of itself. It requires no predetermination nor tight structure. Houle had identified this concept as early as the 1960s in his book, *The Inquiring Mind.*[16]

This type of learning defies the psychological prescription of learning by developmental tasks based upon the individual or the society in which the individual finds himself or herself. New knowledge or skills may be acquired without immediate implications for one's life. Perhaps this is where we truly find the joy of learning.

The difficulty in relation to facilitation of this type of learning is that the learner is truly the only person who can inform us about its requirements. We may be able to determine something about the needs of a couple who are about to be married in relation to the course in marriage preparation. We may predict the occurrence of the need for such a course by consulting social statistics and by observation. Such predictions are no longer applicable when learners defy the system by rising above it.

It will be a joy to work with this adventurous type of learner when we are fortunate enough to encounter him or her. My view is that we are going to meet more learners who do have a greater sense of direction for their learning than is normally found in most groups of learners. It would give me considerable pleasure to think that our activities as religious educators would contribute to the growth of the numbers of persons who learn for the pure joy of the activity.

REFLECTIONS ON TYPES OF LEARNERS

There are persons who learn for the purpose of acquiring new skills and to see themselves grow as persons. Others wish to learn in order to change the world in which they live. Some learners engage in the activity because of the social contact which is involved. There are also those who learn for pure joy. The important thing is to recognize these learners and the specific implications of their involvement with facilitators of adult religious education.

The first group will have a sense of purpose which may come from a sense of vocation to ministry. The most useful thing that one can do to assist this group is to ensure that they truly understand the nature of the vocation. This may occur both before and during the learning process.

A sense of vocation and the faith that the skills can be acquired because of the vocation will provide a committed, conscientious learner. This group will be a pleasure to work with because there is no one more exciting than a confident, motivated learner.

Persons who learn for personal growth do so for internal or internalized reasons which provide their own motivation. The key is for the educator to recognize and respond to these reasons. A lack of response from the educator will mean a lack of participation on the part of the learner. He or she will go where a response is forthcoming.

The need to clarify may be critical to this individual. A careful planning process which takes into consideration the learner's situation will be helpful here. The early stages of the program should include further opportunities for clarifying activities.

Learners for social change have a sense of the need to organize at the outset. The involvement of these learners in the planning process will insure that they have an opportunity to shape the experience in a meaningful way.

If they cannot accomplish their goals through one means, they may choose another. If their goals are in concert with the church's stated goals, we must consider the need to support their efforts in an unqualified manner. For many religious groups, it is appropriate to incorporate social goals within the context of our programs.

This last group of learners, those who learn for the sake of learning, is a delightful group. They have confidence and motivation. They may carry you and other learners along with them in their enthusiasm.

There is, however, a challenge to working with this group. The challenge comes in our ability to help them to find areas in which the learning will be the most beneficial to them. The ability to focus may be a problem which the facilitator can help them to overcome.

Perhaps the most important thing to remember in all of this discussion of the learners is that we should not underestimate them. The forces within learners which involve them in learning vary as much as the shapes and sizes of the learners who come to our activities.

It would be unwise to underestimate the potential for working with many of the learners who come to us. Their capacities and strengths may surprise us, particularly if we take the time to get to know them

Notes

1. K. Patricia Cross, *Adults as Learners* (San Francisco: Jossey-Bass, 1986), p. 1.
2. Ibid., p. 3.
3. Ibid., p. 9.
4. Ibid., p. 28.
5. Ibid., pp. 14-28.
6. Nancy T. Foltz, ed., *Handbook of Adult Religious Education* (Birmingham, Ala.: Religious Education Press, 1986).
7. Sharon B. Merriam and Trenton R. Ferro, "Working with Young Adults," in *Handbook of Adult Religious Education*, ed. Nancy T. Foltz (Birmingham, Ala.: Religious Education Press, 1986).
8. R.E.Y. Wickett, "Working with Middle-Aged Adults," in *Handbook of Adult Religious Education*, ed. Nancy T. Foltz (Birmingham, Ala.: Religious Education Press, 1986).
9. Linda J. Vogel, "Working with Older Adults," in *Handbook of Adult Religious Education*, ed. Nancy T. Foltz (Birmingham, Ala.: Religious Education Press, 1986).
10. James W. White, *Intergenerational Religious Education: Models, Theory, and Prescription for Interage Life and Learning in the Faith Community* (Birmingham, Ala.: Religious Education Press, 1988).
11. Daniel J. Levinson et al., *The Seasons of a Man's Life* (New York: Ballantine Books, 1978), pp. 191-208.
12. Allen Tough, *Why Adults Learn* (Toronto: Ontario Institute for Studies in Education, 1967), p. 10.

13. Ibid., p. 11.

14. Ibid. p. 10.

15. Stephen D. Brookfield, *Understanding and Facilitating Adult Learning* (San Francisco: Jossey-Bass, 1986), p. 99.

16. Cyril O. Houle, *The Inquiring Mind: A Study of the Adult Who Continues to Learn* (Madison: University of Wisconsin Press, 1961).

Chapter 3

The Process of Religious Development

It is critical for the adult religious educator to understand the nature of the process of development which adults undergo in relation to their faith. Some adult educators have found support for their activities in the writings of the developmental psychologists. We should seek to understand the nature of that developmental process as it relates to the religious dimension of the person.

It is important to understand that there is a process of development of the religious component of our being which is related to our physical, psychological, social, and other developmental processes. The examples of development are to be seen everywhere, especially in the lives which are lived around each one of us. The writings of our various traditions tell us of growth and developmental experiences ranging from the relatively rapid conversion of the Christian, St. Paul, to the slow but steady increase in knowledge and understanding of the ancient, scholarly religious.

One of the difficulties of determining the nature of the growth which occurs as a result of our religious development involves the different ways in which religions define themselves and the processes which are a part of the defined religion. Both religion and culture are important components to consider when we examine the nature of religious development.

This book is written primarily with a North American context in mind. The majority of readers will be functioning as educators within that context. We should, nevertheless, be prepared to accept the differences which will occur through the presence of others who bring their culture and religious beliefs to us in this world.

Because our definitions of the developmental process are wide indeed, we need to consider those definitions which will be most helpful. One of the most useful definitions for adult religious educators can be found in the work of James Fowler.[1] Fowler's writings consider the process of "faith development" through the utilization of psycho-social developmental processes.

Fowler describes faith as the aspect of our being which makes sense out of chaos and provides us with meaning.[2] It is a helpful definition if we wish to see the connection between personality development and faith development. I am not certain that this will satisfy the theologians, but it will be of value to educators who seek a "holistic" definition of the person.

The reason why this is a valuable definition for those who wish to make a connection between personality development and faith development is because certain recent authors from the field of developmental psychology have indicated that one's value system (or faith, if you prefer) is a part of the developing personality. Daniel Levinson[3] and other psychologists of the 1980s appear to support this point of view.

Levinson's definition of a mid-life change or transition contains elements which could constitute a form of faith system.[4] If people are to attempt to come to terms with their lives during this eventful period, they need to consider the basic system of values, beliefs, and attitudes which has shaped their lives to that point in time. If a mid-life transition does nothing else, it will involve the reexamination of these fundamental components of personality.

Roger Gould[5] suggests that this is an important aspect of personality development at an earlier stage as well. He sees it as a part of the transitional stage of the late twenties and early thirties during which people experience a lesser transition than the so-called mid-life crisis. Personal values, attitudes, and beliefs are considered in this period with resulting adjustments for some persons according to Gould.[6]

A theologian, James Loder, has provided us with insight as to the manner transitions can be seen to take place. His concept of the "transforming moment" provides a basis for understanding the concept of transition. Loder states that "this prominent aspect of development is transformational in its basic pattern."[7] He defines the "transformation" as "designating a change in form from lower to higher orders of life along a line of continuous development.[8]

Loder relates the process of transformation to the way we begin to "know" things. It is the process of "convictional knowing" that leads to transformation. The involvement of the Holy Spirit is clear in his definition of this deeper way of knowing. He states, "Convictional knowing is the patterned process by which the Holy Spirit transforms all transformations of the human spirit."[9] It is most important for us to remember that the learning process which may lead to, or support convictional knowing, is not solely in the hands of the educator or facilitator.

Another theologian has expressed a definition of spiritual development which brings us quite close to the psychologists' definitions. Paul Tillich describes the concept of spiritual self-affirmation in his book, *The Courage to Be*.[10] According to this author, the process or spiritual self-affirmation involves the search for the meaning of life.[11] It might be suggested that one can affirm one's very being by the search for meaning.

Tillich's concept is valuable in that it reinforces the relationship between what the modern psychologist is saying and what the theologian is saying. Both groups have focused on an essential element of the person.

The many works of Erik Erikson provide us with valuable insight into personality development during the adult years. Erikson has divided the process into what are called "the eight ages." Two important aspects of the developmental process for this author involve a single, major focus for the development in each age and the implications of earlier ages of development on later ages.[12]

The most recent work on Eriksonian theory confirms the importance of this latter aspect. Erikson himself reports in a recent interview about the impact of earlier development on the older adult.[13] Don Browning writes in his book, *The Generative Man*,[14] about the impact of earlier periods upon middle adulthood.

Another well-known writer on personality development describes the importance of development from the period of childhood to that of adulthood. Roger Could describes the way we move away from "unwarranted expectations, rigid rules and inflexible rules. It is in this way, according to Gould, that we become "owners of our own selves."[15] The parallel to Fowler's development of faith where we begin to seek and to have our own answers to the vital questions of our faith is clear.

There are certain aspects of personality development which should be considered by the reader. Both moral development and cognitive development are important components of personality development which will impact upon aspects of faith. The relationship between the development of morals, attitudes, and values and faith development can be seen as almost axiomatic. The level of cognitive development can be linked also to our level of faith development.

One of the most influential psychologists in the area of cognitive development is Jean Piaget. This researcher's writing should be reviewed because it contains a consideration of the progress of thinking from the most rudimentary levels to the most complex level of abstract thinking.

The danger of a description of cognitive development by Piaget or any other cognitive theorist is that we may begin to apply it to all adults. It should be clear to all who work with adult learners that not every learner will achieve the most complex levels of abstract thinking.

Lawrence Kohlberg's writings on moral development have influenced Fowler's understanding of the process of faith development in a rather profound manner. This author's three levels, each one with two manifestations, parallels Fowler's six stages of faith.[16]

Fowler's work has shown us one way to interrelate the developmental process of the personality with the growth and development of the faith component of our being. The strength of Fowler's model lies precisely in his choice of aspects of the personality as the supporting structure for faith development.[17]

The following table is a compilation of various aspects of the process of faith development. The origins of the table may be found in the various writings about the faith developmental process by Fowler and other authors.

TABLE 1

	FOWLER (Stages)	PIAGET (Form of Logic)	KOHLBERG (Form of Moral Judgment)	ERIKSON (Eight Ages)	LEVINSON (Seasons)
INFANCY 0 - 1 ½ / 2	Undifferentiated	Sensorimotor		Basic Trust/ Mistrust	
EARLY CHILDHOOD 2 - 6	Intuitive-Projective Faith	Preoperational	Preconventional	Autonomy/Shame	
CHILDHOOD 7 - 12	Mythic-Literal Faith	Concerete Operational		Industry/ Inferiority	
ADOLESCENCE 13 - 21	Synthetic-Conventional Faith	Formal Operational	Conventional	Identity/ Role Confusion	Early Adult 17 Transition
YOUNG ADULTHOOD 21 - 35	Individuative-Reflective Faith		Postconventional	Intimacy/ Isolation	Age 30 Transition
MIDDLE ADULTHOOD 35 - 60	Conjunctive Faith			Generativity/ Stagnation	Mid-Life Transition
OLDER ADULTHOOD 60 +	Universalizing			Integrity/ Despair	Late-Adult Transition

Another author who has described a process of development which is worthy of consideration by the educator is Henri Nouwen. One reason why this author is of importance to the educator may be found within the three dimensions of his spiritual growth process. Nouwen writes about the search which occurs within each individual for the spiritual dimension of the self, the search which involves the spiritual dimension of others, and the search which occurs in direct relationship with God.[18]

The value of Nouwen's work is found in its combination of the individual and the social parts of the being in relation to God. We can define ourselves as persons separate from others in a manner which does not parallel but speaks to the same issue as Erikson's Identity Age of adolescents who are becoming adults. The social side may be seen in relation to the Intimacy and Generative Stages of young and middle adulthood. The Stage of Ego Integrity is reached in later adulthood when one has a sense of wholeness which involves the need to relate to God.

As educators we may find ways of assisting people in each one of Nouwen's dimensions or phases. People clearly wish to receive support from others as they engage in the second dimension. The support which occurs in relation to the first and second dimension is less clear, but equally valuable at times. The value of the experience of others in the search for self-understanding is comprehended by all travelers on the journey. Similarly, we may utilize the experience others have in relation to God in order to explore the nature of our own relationship.

Our own insecurity as facilitators may push us to intervene at moments when it is inappropriate. There are times when the searcher looks inside or to God, and we should not presume to intervene. The best approach may be silence or expressed support for individual searching.

Perhaps the best approach of all is to see the individuality of the developmental process. All theories of note have been accepted because they contain some truth concerning the reality which they attempt to describe. The fact is that social and psychological theories do change from time to time with new discoveries and a changing society. No human theorists have been able to describe totally the human condition for all time. What theorists give us is some assistance in understanding aspects of the human condition at particular points in time. We must use the insight gained from this assistance while acknowledging both its contribution to understanding and its limitations.

Each person seeks meaning for the self in a manner which is personally related. This may be done in a framework of a religion or a philosophy, but it always speaks to the person in relation to his or her own life. This is a process where we can but share the journey in a positive and supportive manner. It will be impossible for us to interfere with the individual and the deeper part of his or her being. We would be unwise to do so, but it is possible to support the positive journey of the spirit.

The question of the role of other persons, either individually or in a group should be considered in relation to this individual experience of growth and learning. We have long contended that the group provides the supportive environment where the individual can achieve appropriate goals.

If the individual can best learn within a safe environment, as adult educators such as Kidd[19] and Knowles[20] have suggested, the religious group should aim to create the environment within which the personal goal can be achieved

SUMMARY

The most essential component of this approach to adult religious education is found in the relationship of the spiritual aspect of the person and the totality of the person. These cannot be separated. They must be examined holistically as interwoven aspects of the same being.

The problem we must overcome is to describe the spiritual aspect in a manner which has integrity in and of itself while maintaining the integrity of the holistic approach. The psychological approach which involves both the society and the physical aspects in relation to development enables this integration to be maintained.

We draw, as do our colleagues in adult education, upon the work of the developmental psychologists from the socio-psychological orientation. Society is considered to be of major importance to this group which includes such authors as Erikson and Levinson, but the influence of the physical developmental process is considered by this group also.

Notes

1. James W. Fowler, *Stages of Faith: The Psychology of Human Development and the Quest for Meaning* (San Francisco: Harper & Row, 1981).

2. Ibid. p. 33, and James W. Fowler, "Faith and the Structuring of Meaning," in *Faith Development and Fowler*, ed. Craig Dykstra and Sharon Parks (Birmingham, Ala.: Religious Education Press, 1986).

3. Daniel J. Levinson, *The Seasons of a Man's Life* (New York: Ballantine Books, 1978).

4. Ibid. pp. 49-52.

5. Roger L. Gould, *Transformations: Growth and Change in Adult Life* (New York: Simon and Schuster, 1978).

6. Ibid., pp. 153-154.

7. James E. Loder, *The Transformational Moment: Understanding Convictional Experiences* (San Francisco: Harper & Row, 1981), p. 129.

8. Ibid., p. 38.

9. Ibid., p. 92.

10. Paul Tillich, *The Courage to Be* (New Haven: Yale University Press, 1952).

11. Ibid., p. 49.

12. Erik Erikson, *Childhood and Society*, 2nd ed. (New York: Norton, 1963), chapter 7.

13. *New York Times*, June, 1988.

14. Don S. Browning, *Generative Man: Psychoanalytical Perspectives* (Philadelphia: Westminster, 1972).

15. Gould, *Transformations: Growth and Change in Adult Life*, p. 37.

16. Fowler, *Stages of Faith: The Psychology of Human Development and the Quest for Meaning*, p. 52, and "Faith and the Structuring of Meaning," p. 34.

17. Fowler, "Faith and the Structuring of Meaning," pp. 31-37.

18. Henri Nouwen, *Reaching Out: The Three Movements of the Spiritual Life* (Garden City, N.Y.: Doubleday, 1975).

19. James R. Kidd, *How Adults Learn*, rev. ed. (New York: Cambridge Press, 1973), pp. 107-108.

20. Malcolm S. Knowles, *The Modern Practice of Adult Education: Pedagogy versus Andragogy* (Houston: Gulf Publishing, 1970), pp. 46-47.

Chapter 4

Philosophical Issues In Adult Religious Education

The reasons why people come to adult education institutions are numerous and have been well documented. When asked for reasons why they attend, there will be a round of predictable answers including ones about certification, long-held interests, sociability, and the filling of leisure time.

In addition to formal education opportunities, education and learning happen continually in people's lives, and people would be in serious difficulties if learning were limited only to what was taught in educational institutions. Educational activities can be found in the ongoing, nonstructured, and incidental events in day-to-day existence. The ways in which we continue to learn and engage in questions surrounding these events are specific to us as individuals and are most revealing of who we are as people.

The conjunction of adult education and adult religious education is not immediately obvious to those who limit their definition of education to the activities which happen in formal educational institutions. Similarly limited is a view of religious education which permits only those topics with specific religious application. The narrow training of subject matter specialists can prohibit the understanding that adult religious education is capable of addressing the fundamental needs of the whole person and not some compartmentalized version. Through the conjunction of education and religious experience, adults come to explore some of the most profound questions touching their humanity.

Both fields are capable of helping people raise questions about what it is to be human, about how we are called into being, and about how we engage in a response in the way we live our lives which is appropriate to our revised calling. Surely adult religious educators would wish nothing less for people than that their lives would be free of distortion and the oppression that binds them and prevents them in a spiritual sense from the realization of who they are. It is in this light that Paulo Freire speaks of education as the "practice of freedom" as opposed to the "practice of domination."[1]

One reason people join religious institutions and, indeed, leave them if this is not satisfied, is to find some integration of their personal and spiritual lives. Some of the theories of adult development suggest that this integration is a very present need as people strive for personal fulfillment in their lives. Theorists have described this need in a variety of ways. Phrases such as Erikson's "ego integrity vs. despair,"[2] Whitehead's "wisdom,"[3] Maslow's "self-actualization,"[4] Westerhoff's "owned faith,"[5] and Fowler's "universalizing faith"[6] describe the final stages of adult development in the respective theories.

The human activity of becoming is the focus of both educators and religious leaders. This is especially true for the latter when the process of becoming includes one's spirituality in the definition of what it means to be a human being.

Whatever specific reasons people have for searching out religious institutions, the reasons are not likely to be disinterested. As in other educational settings, those who seek religious guidance are responding to the desire to satisfy some need. Religious leaders may come to know and even anticipate some of the needs of their community, for the needs will be many. The task of knowing all the needs is, of course, impossible, especially because some people are themselves incapable of expressing their motivation. Adult education theories are useful for understanding some aspects of adult development, and two are mentioned here only briefly.

Maslow's "Hierarchy of Human Needs" includes at one extreme our most basic need for physical safety and extends to the other extreme, to our need for self-actualization. Just as the needs of the community will change from time to time, so will the needs for any individual. An example familiar to religious leaders is the kind of support they are called on to provide in times of crisis such as a sudden death when predictable patterns of behavior are taken over by unprecedented requests for nurture and support. An educator who is aware of the wide variety of needs in any learning community will not be surprised when a particular education program is met with an equally wide variety of responses.

A theory of needs may explain why a program initiated by learners is more successful than a program initiated by the institution. Organizations will more closely meet the needs of their members when opportunities are provided for participation in the direction and planning of activities. In spite of the many things which could be taught and the eagerness of the adult religious educator to impart knowledge to learners, educational events will be dull and uninspiring when answers are given to questions which have not been asked or for which there is no expressed need. Successful programs will be about the real concerns and issues in the present, concrete, personal and social lives of participants.

Another issue of critical importance in this chapter is the nature of faith and its role in relation to religion and the adult religious educator. According to James Michael Lee, faith is an aspect of religion. Faith involves the way people "organize and implement their lives as persons."[7] Most reasonable definitions of the nature of a religion would be much broader than this. Lee sees faith as being a necessary component but not sufficient for religion.[8]

Adult development can be characterized according to individual stages of faith development as described by James Fowler.[9] Fowler's definition of faith could be described as a verb. It is a cognitive action which evolves from one stage to another by a dialectical process. Understanding these cognitive-based faith stages may be useful in program planning in helping to avoid a presentation that is either too complex or too rudimentary for the participants.

Of even greater use to the adult religious educator is that Fowler's six stages of faith development refer not only to the individual but also to the faith community.[10] That is, a community of believers can be characterized by the normative stance it takes regarding its collective faith. If most of the believers are at Fowler's third stage of synthetic conventional faith the community will generally be at the same stage. This happens, not just because of the sway of the majority but because the community has collectively created and continues to hold the faith by which it calls itself into existence. It is in a faith community consisting of as few as two people where individuals come to the knowledge and practice of their faith. But because faith is a shared experience, according to Fowler, it is not surprising that individuals rarely get beyond the faith development of the community, for it is in community where they receive support and are able to identify with what they believe.

Fowler's definition of faith may be related to a broader definition of faith as seen in the writing of V. Bailley Gillespie.[11] Like Fowler, Gillespie believes that faith evolves developmentally.[12] Faith can be seen as related to an experience which brings the person closer to God, and, because we can support such experience, there are implications for the adult religious educator as someone who is part of the learner's experience.[13]

Gillespie's comment that faith is relational is important. There is an "object" in faith relationships, thus allowing us to be faithful to someone or something.[14] This aspect of faith is also seen in Fowler's writings.[15]

The development of faith is a shared experience created, in part, through dialogue with members of the faith community. The value of dialogue is judged according to how it assists in the developmental process of making moral and rational judgments. This is not accomplished merely by the sharing of objective knowledge but by the action or interaction of two subjects who create knowledge and understanding anew between them. By the interaction with religious teachings and interpretation with others in the faith community, learners come to understand the meaning of their faith.

Through communicative action participants do much more than exchange information. They create their own understanding and interpret the topic under discussion in light of their own life experiences. Both as a group and individually, participants have an interest in examining critically the curriculum, message, or agenda of the institution they attend. Initially they will be interested in deciding whether or not the message is right and true. But ultimate appropriation of the message occurs when the participant not only raises the question "Is it true?" but "Is it true for me?" Participants will come to know both theoretically and in terms of their own existence the difference between the false view that distorts relationships and the message that rings true under careful examination.

Through reflection and dialogue, we learn to question and examine critically the information which is presented to us. It is in communication with others and the message and not just through solitary self-reflection that understanding is reached. In a dialectical relationship with others we share ideas, create knowledge, and come to be who we are. Through critical inquiry and dialogue we move to uncover distortions found in our own thoughts and actions and those of society. We can collectively examine and discover systems of domination that prevent us from coming to an understanding of ourselves, each other, and the topic at hand.

Distortions occur not only in our understanding of issues and topics but also in the way the topic is discussed. Through critical inquiry and self-reflection, we work to free the communication process from the distortions that come from many sides—including ideology that binds, methodology that has become truth, and structure that no longer serves us. Predetermined answers, false rhetoric, and pat solutions are unacceptable to the process because they circumvent the need for personal involvement. Because institutions largely control the issues that may be raised to the level of consciousness, educators of religious institutions would do well to be aware of the codes, both named and unnamed, operating within their communities which determine the agenda and the way it will be discussed. Member involvement does not happen at the end of a monologue merely by the call of the speaker for questions.

Communication with learners is not just to assure the leader that the message is "getting across." Rather, communication is an open invitation to the learner to form and perhaps to voice for the first time what he or she understands. The power of language is such that we must sometimes verbalize what we know in order to understand it.

Participants need to be invited to share their stories and name their personal experiences. This naming is not just for interest sake or because it is a good ice breaker. It enables participants to acknowledge their humanness as something in common with others present. In moving beyond this sharing of stories, participants are further involved in the next step which is to reflect critically on the topic at hand.

Many strategies or teaching models exist which promote reflection and dialogue among participants. Although the strategies may start simply with questions of factual detail, the most successful processes involve questions requiring critical reflection, especially when questions are raised by the participants themselves. According to Thomas Groome, it is in this way that participants are able to consider the important questions: "Why we do what we do and what [are] our hopes in doing it?"[16]

Paulo Freire writes extensively on the promotion of critical consciousness ("conscientization") in education. Reflection on one's historical experience that gives rise to actions is essential to Freire's praxis approach. According to Freire, pedagogues who believe that education is to be an exercise in freedom will act "with" rather than "over" people, enabling them to name their own world and, through dialogue, come to action and faith. Those participants engaged in the dialectical process are already involved in revolutionary praxis. The emancipatory interest[17] is satisfied anew by the continual engagement of the personal in the intersubjective creation of knowledge and meaning.

THE DIALOGUE

Because of the overarching importance of dialogue in the educative process, it may be useful to clarify an understanding of the terms, "dialogue" and "dialectic." As they have been used so far, dialogue and dialectic are roughly synonymous. One common understanding of the latter is of a continual conversation that is forever open and forever moving in a back-and-forth motion between the two partners in a conversation. It is in the process of elaborating one position after the other that an understanding takes place between them. Dialectical understanding continually changes as the participants evolve in their appropriation of the material.

Hegel's concept of the dialectic includes the idea of the Spirit, although it should be made clear that his view of the Spirit would differ from that of theologians.[18] This three-sided concept is clearly a negation of the dualism of earlier philosophy. James Michael Lee suggests that Hegel's "predilection" for triads seems to have some derivation in the concept of the Trinity.[19]

Whereas "dialectic" is the process of a continually evolving speech situation, "dialogue" is the name of the event. In a more casual understanding of the idea of dialogue, we may easily come to expect less than the dynamic creation of meaning predicted above. It is easy to see that very little under-standing occurs when a dialogue is actually two alternating monologues. Neither is dialogue occurring or even pretending to occur in the description of education that Freire calls the "banking" concept. When the educator in the role of narrator does the thinking, talking, choosing, and acting, students are relegated to perform the role of "containers" to be "filled" by the teach-er. Instead of engaging in the experience of learning, students become the recipients of information; knowledge is transferred but not created.[20]

In contrast to the banking concept is Freire's "problem-posing" idea which calls for personal and critical engagement in one's own learning. Whereas in banking education where students are required only to nod in agreement and repeat what they are told, the problem-posing concept cannot help but involve students in a conscious examination of the facts as they relate to the students' lives. Problems posed by the students challenge them to create solutions from their own experiences drawn from the world and their faith community. This will enable them to affirm who they are and transform themselves through the posing of problems.[21]

While there is no formula for education, adult learning is not likely to hap-pen without the integral component of participants' reflection on their own experiences. Through dialogue and the sharing of experiences, participants hear each others' stories, make connections in their own lives, and appro-priate the knowledge generated in the exchange. The taking hold of one's faith in a way that makes it possible for a person to act on it happens, as far as human intervention is concerned, when the faith is informed by its par-ticular tradition and personally appropriated in the context of lived faith experience. Beyond individual knowing, participants have an opportunity to reflect on what the community holds to be true and what their faith looks like in action.

THE EDUCATOR

There will be those adult religious educators whose natural inclinations, training, and personalities are more comfortable with a structured approach to education, one that has hints and suggestions for "how to get people to dis-cuss things" even if it is only for the five minutes remaining after a "talk." The genius of Freire's emphasis on problem posing is that it implies self-reflec-tion for the leader at least as much as for the participants. Leaders willing to examine the distortion of power in a teaching/learning situation will find that the structure of their teaching will constantly change.

As participants assume more responsibility for their own learning, the leader's role will require flexibility and openness to a leadership style that extends well beyond the role granted by traditional authority. The vertical structure of teacher to learner is undermined by problem-posing education as the educator engages in a reconsideration of previously held positions in the light of new student exchanges.

The banking concept of education insures that the separate roles of teacher and student are strictly maintained, and dialectic educators who rely on the authority of their positions will not feel comfortable with Freire's ideas about what education can be. His strongest appeal, however, is that education is the practice of freedom from oppression on all sides. By engaging in problem posing of their own, leaders are no longer merely filling a role, but are engaging in learning of their own, not the least of which is what it means to be with people who are struggling to create meaning. When the leader is a co-learner, the learners are in a better position to be co-leaders who mutually support each other in their learning projects. When the faith community experiences its own ability to support its members, the knowledge of that ability is empowering.

The connection between understanding and doing must speak to educators about engaging in thoughtful practice. Similarly, no educator can expect participants to learn well without the opportunity to express themselves in active participation. Religious leaders are required not only to have an understanding of the theory or doctrine of their religion but also to be good practitioners of it; their faith will be demonstrated in actions as well as words. In this way they have something more than theological scholarship to share; their experience will also be a part of the faith community.

Sometimes an adult religious educator will make the largest contribution to members of the faith community by getting out of their way and letting people get on with their own learning. More specifically, a religious educator can help people clear away some of the barriers that inhibit learning, barriers such as satisfaction with pat answers, reluctance to raise questions, and fear at admitting doubts.

Adult religious educators are also learners when they actively engage with participants in the reflection, research, and systematic investigation of their call to faith.

Notes

1. Paulo Freire, *Pedagogy of the Oppressed* (New York: Seabury, 1969).

2. Erik Erikson, *Childhood and Society* (New York: Norton, 1950).

3. Evelyn Whitehead and James Whitehead, *Christian Life Patterns: The Psychological Challenges and Religious Invitations of Adult Life* (New York: Doubleday, 1979).

4. A.H. Maslow, *Motivation and Personality* (New York: Harper and Brothers, 1970).

5. John H. Westerhoff III, *Will our Children Have Faith?* (New York: Seabury, 1976).

6. James W. Fowler, *Stages of Faith: The Psychology of Human Development and the Quest for Meaning* (San Francisco: Harper & Row, 1981).

7. James Michael Lee, "The Authentic Source of Religious Instruction," in *Religious Education and Theology*, ed. Norma H. Thompson (Birmingham, Ala.: Religious Education Press, 1982), p. 107.

8. Ibid., p. 101.

9. For a complete description, see Fowler, *Stages of Faith*, pp. 119-213.

10. Ibid., pp. 294-296.

11. V. Bailley Gillespie, *The Experience of Faith* (Birmingham, Ala.: Religious Education Press, 1988).

12. Ibid., p. 6.

13. Ibid., pp. 20-21.

14. Ibid., p. 28.

15. James W. Fowler, "Faith and the Structuring Of Meaning," in *Faith Development and Fowler*, ed. Craig Dykstra and Sharon Parks, (Birmingham, Ala.: Religious Education Press, 1986), pp. 16-19.

16. Thomas H. Groome, *Christian Religious Education: Sharing our Story and Vision* (San Francisco: Harper & Row, 1980), p. 211.

17. Jürgen Habermas, *Knowledge and Human Interest* (Boston: Beacon, 1971).

18. John Plamenatz, *Man and Society: A Critical Examination of Some Important Social and Political Theories from Machiavelli to Marx,* Volume II (London: Longmans, 1963), p. 136.

19. Lee, "The Authentic Source of Religious Instruction," p. 167.

20. Freire, *Pedagogy of the Oppressed*, p. 59.

21. Ibid., pp. 66-74.

Chapter 5

How To Choose A Model

Choices of models are made for a variety of reasons when it comes to the provision of adult religious education programs. The most frequent reason would appear to be personal preference on the part of the facilitator, but familiarity is often an important factor. We use the models and facilitative procedures which have worked for us in the past. There is clearly an inclination toward the "tried and true." We must, however, insure that the limits of our own experience do not constrict us unduly.

The development of an educational model is based in part on our experiences in the educational context and a theoretical base. The definition of a theory, as presented in Webster's dictionary, contains the statements that a theory is "the analysis of a set of facts in their relation to one another" and "a belief, policy, or procedure proposed or followed as the basis of action."[1] Both aspects of the meaning of the word are important to us in the context first of understanding then acting accordingly.

Effective models are derived from sound theory and thoughtful practice. They exemplify the concept of "praxis" as demonstrated by the work of Paulo Freire and described by authors such as Thomas Groome.[2] The models in this volume find their roots in theory and the rest of the body continues to grow and evolve from the base. The shape of the model is related to its environment as well as the base or roots.

It is important to remember that a model is selected as a framework for action. It should be used to guide the action which will take place involving the educator and learner or learners. It is a base for action which is derived from both theory and practice.

If there is one good reason for trying an alternative approach to the facilitation of learning, we should consider the possible alternatives carefully

34

before we reject them. Our repertoire may be too limited. We owe the careful consideration of alternatives to the learners who require our assistance.

The following factors must be reviewed in order to make an appropriate decision concerning the selection of a model. They will vary in the weight of their implications for the decision-making process but they need to be considered in each case. These factors include the nature of the learner or learners, the content area to be learned, the resources which are required, the context in which the learning will occur, and of the facilitator or facilitators who will be involved. I shall review each area in turn.

THE NATURE OF THE LEARNER

The primary consideration in virtually all circumstances will be the nature of the learner or learners who will participate in the learning activity. Adult education has survived for many years as an activity of choice because adult educators have not forgotten this factor.

The axiom of "knowing the learner" will assist the facilitator to avoid unnecessary errors, ineffective decisions, and inappropriate activities. The results will be seen in effective learning and positive feelings toward the learning process.

There are certain characteristics of learners which will assist us to know how to work appropriately with them. Maturity, experience, and social orientation are among the factors which motivate learners to pursue their learning on a continuous basis.

Malcolm Knowles emphasizes the maturity and experience of learners in his assumptions of andragogy,[3] but there is no indication that these qualities are to be found in equal amounts in all learners. I believe that there is evidence in Knowles' work to suggest that adults change and grow during the life span as we see in his references to Havighurst and other developmental psychologists.[4]

There is a clear suggestion in Knowles' writings that certain assumptions can be made about some adult learners but not all adult learners. His books on learning contracts indicate that certain characteristics should be considered before the contract is chosen as an option.[5] These characteristics include direct reference to the learner's experience, skill, and interest in relation to the learning. He does not take these characteristics as given for all adult learners.

Another issue which should be considered is the extent to which people wish to be dependent or independent in their approach to learning. This has been described as "field dependence" and "field independence" in the literature of education and psychology.[6] The key issue here is that field dependent learners will rely more on other persons and structure in order to accomplish their goals.

It is not difficult to recognize field dependent people insofar as their dependency is a characteristic of their overall personality and recognizable as such. If you have learners who rely on others regularly and indicate a need for structure in other areas of their lives, they will approach learning in a manner consistent with this personality trait.

The skills the learner has may be a major factor in the decision to utilize a particular model. The ability to function individually in a self-directed model will mean that the learner must have or must acquire certain skills. A learner who wants to have direct access to information will need to know how to access that information.

The ability to function independently must be combined with a certain ability to analyze and to identify needs, goals and objectives, resources, and an appropriate plan to pursue. I suggest that a certain ability is required because the learner can receive support from the facilitator during the process. New skills may be acquired during the interactions while problems are being solved.

The skills may be acquired in group settings where there is a support system in place and a resource person to assist in the process of acquisition. An alternative solution may be to work with an individual to develop the requisite skills. Once the skills are acquired, they will serve the learner for many learning activities. Should the facilitator wish to establish a more objective perspective on the skills of the potential self-directed learner, an instrument such as the Self-Directed Learning Readiness Scale of Lucy Guglielmino[7] may be employed.

THE NATURE OF THE SUBSTANTIVE CONTENT

We can divide the substantive content to be learned into a variety of categories, but the most frequently cited division for educators has included reference to the celebrated three-volume works on taxonomy of educational objectives written or inspired by Benjamin Bloom.[8] This approach to the division of learning recognizes the diversity of facilitative procedures be used in our attempts to reach quite different types of goals.

Bloom's taxonomies refer to the basic areas of learning as related to the cognitive or knowledge domain, the affective domain, and the psychomotor domain. Although there are many times when we are concerned with all three areas in relation to a particular learning activity, these divisions allow us to organize the learning into appropriate aspects.

One extremely valuable approach to the understanding of content can be found in the writing of James Michael Lee. This analysis of content is applied quite directly to the field of religious education in his book, *The Content of Religious Instruction*.[9] Lee suggests that there are nine "discreet and distinct contents" which together form the substantive content which is an essential component of the content of religious instruction.[10] The nine contents are as follows:

1. product content
2. process content
3. cognitive content
4. affective content
5. verbal content
6. nonverbal content
7. conscious content
8. unconscious content
9. lifestyle content[11]

It is quite obvious that these content areas often represent two sides of a situation, hence they are placed within four groups with lifestyle content as an individual area. The pairs are: 1) product/process; 2) cognitive/affective; 3) verbal/nonverbal; and 4) conscious/unconscious.[12]

Lee suggests further that there is a direct relationship between substantive content and facilitational procedures which precludes the necessity of erecting a false dichotomy between the two.[13] There is a considerable amount of truth in this statement, although I think that some educators in their stress on content as primarily "academic" have, unfortunately, created this false dichotomy.

It can be suggested that the learning of knowledge or factual information differs substantively from the learning of skills or attitudes or values. The process by which knowledge is acquired may involve such activities as memorization and cognitive integration. Skills are often learned by practice and repetition. Perhaps the most difficult area of all is the area of attitudes and values where feelings and existing attitudes may be examined through experience and reflection.

There are times when the substantive content to be learned is flexible. The option to respond to the learner's suggestions or identified interests should be considered here. Where the content to be learned is specified for certain reasons such as certification, the possibility for flexibility is lessened. It is still necessary to insure that the learning experience is related to the learner's experience and knowledge base in order to maximize the potential for learning.

Our expectations of the models to assist us to enable the learner and the facilitator to work with different areas of content are considerable. There is a need, however, to consider the fact that models are often more adaptable than limited. One model may be used for different content areas with expectations of success.

When we have said that models may be quite adaptable, this does not mean to suggest that certain models do not prove to be more successful in some substantive content areas while less successful in others. We need to consider each model to determine where and how it can be used in order to insure the maximum level of potential success.

The models which are described in this volume are able to facilitate learning for knowledge, attitudes, and lifestyle behavior. Several models are used extensively to promote learning for cognitive content. Some models have proven to be particularly useful in the learning of lifestyle. The affective domain receives the impact of most forms of learning in that our attitudes are affected frequently when we learn something.

The area of the affective domain gives many adult educators difficulty when they move beyond its surface. The issue of sensitivity arises when we presume to intervene in this highly personal dimension. On the other hand, how can we expect people to learn and grow without change in this dimension of their being?

The difficulty must be faced. We must determine when and how it is permissible to work with learners in this area. It is my view that we must be able to work with them if we wish to achieve any success. There is also a feeling I have which suggests that we, as educators, should be prepared to be influenced in this area as well. If we are not open to this possibility, we should not suggest the possibility to other mature, responsible persons.

The need for the skills of ministry is known throughout the religious institution. Many may participate in the ministry, but the requirement should always be for "skillful" ministry. These skills will be learned in various settings, but they will be learned in part within the religious community itself. We must offer people the support which is required to exercise their ministry and that support will include training.

Perhaps the most important aspect of content is that which combines knowledge, skill, and attitudes. I am referring to the content of lifestyle, as described by Nancy Foltz in her chapter in *The Handbook of Adult Religious Education*.[14] If this area of lifestyle is changed through learning in all three domains, we shall need to seek models that are good for all three in order to assist the learner to grow in this critical aspect.

Which models should be used for which areas or domains of learning? I suggest that it may be best to identify the specific individual model's strengths and weaknesses as is required in relation to each domain rather than indicate limited usage of a model for one domain. This will be done in the chart in the latter part of this chapter and in each chapter.

THE NATURE OF THE RESOURCE BASE

We must be realistic about those resources which learners will need to proceed with the learning activity and those resources which are available to assist in the process. We should consider both the human resources and the variety of other resources available to us. We do this in a world which has created a multiplicity of ways for us to access those resources. ,

A review of the educational goals and objectives for a plan or program will enable us to determine exactly what types of resources are required for learning. The specific nature of the resources used should be identified in part for the learner, but there is a certain advantage in all but isolated situations to have the learner search for resources.

It is possible for us to be creative in our search for resources. We should consider the alternatives including all possible media of communications. Books are so familiar to most of us that we tend to consider them first. Other media do provide accessible alternatives such as videotapes and films, records and tapes, and the computerized network of information.

The computer will allow us to access not only each other but vast networks of stored materials. We can "pull out" material from the machine over the telephone lines far more easily than from the library bookshelf. The future cost and time involved in electronic communication will mean that interaction with resource persons and materials at a distance will be extremely easy. A computer with printer and modem plus a telephone line will become essential for many educators in the near future.

Each learning activity will require specific resources. They must be identified on an individual basis with a creative, responsible approach. They can be identified cooperatively by the facilitator and learner or learners, but the need to identify them for successful learning activities should not be in doubt.

THE SITUATIONAL CONTEXT OF LEARNING

What is possible may be dictated to a certain extent by the context in which the learning is expected to take place. Certain communities or institutions, whether ecclesiastical or secular, will have expectations about how learning should take place and what is suitable for learning in religious education. To move outside of these expectations is often possible but only after considerable thought and planning has occurred.

Know the situation and the expectations of the community and the learners prior to the planning and provision of programs. When these factors have been identified, create the situation in which successful innovation is more probable than the failure.

The plans and priorities of the institutions within which many religious educators work will have an impact upon our plans and activities. They will create expectations among facilitators and learners alike. These institutions may have rules, norms, and attitudes which limit choice. I am not prepared to suggest that you attempt to challenge these institutional limits or that you abide by them without thought. You may feel that the learners require challenge but you should never attempt to challenge without the full knowledge of the implications of such action.

Should you plan to be innovative, insure that there is sufficient support in the situation to warrant the movement into the innovation. Local leadership and opinion makers can assist in securing the success of an innovation.

Should your plans involve a standard approach to the field of adult religious education, knowledge of the context of learning will still be useful in the planning and implementation stages. The more information you have, the greater the likelihood of success.

THE FACILITATOR

I use this as a term for those persons who assist the learner or learners to learn in a variety of ways. These ways may include direct involvement in a teaching-learning process as well as the type of involvement which is less direct. Planning is an obvious activity which does facilitate learning, but evaluative activity may also be seen as facilitative. Any person who does these things is a facilitator by my definition.

It has always been my view that the facilitator should "know" the act of learning adequately in order to be successful. The good facilitator should know how learning can be best performed and how one feels during the process. This can be accomplished by an examination of one's own learning and by discussion with others about their experiences. Many adult religious educators will have acquired the requisite skills to perform these "examinations" through their prior education and training.

After one has a sense of learning, it is important to consider the nature of the relationships with learners which are most compatible for the facilitator. The extent to which one shares responsibility for learning will be a critical issue in this respect. If I am uncomfortable with a lack of contact with learners, I may prefer to avoid involvement in distance education situations. If I prefer to work in group settings, I may wish to do more of my work in those group situations. If I like to work in situations where responsibility is shared with all parties to the learning, I shall be more open to working in self-directed situations.

Do what you do best as often as possible in the interests of the learner or learners. Be flexible, insofar as it is possible, to enable learning in situations where your preferred approach is not the best for the circumstances. Avoid those situations where you feel very uncomfortable or incompatible with the approach to learning that learners require. Situations where you are extremely uncomfortable will not have positive results for you or the learners. Allow someone else to assume the responsibility where needed.

A SHORT REVIEW OF THE MODELS

Each model has its place in the system based upon its strengths and weaknesses. Both the traditional and alternative models are appropriate under certain circumstances but may not work in others. The following comments will assist in the reader's understanding of some factors which will affect the decision about when to use each model.

The traditional, andragogical models (see chapters 6 to 9) work well with all three categories of content at both the basic and advanced levels and with the average adult learner in a group. They will be suited to most religious institutions within our communities.

These models are flexible enough to allow various types of activities under their general umbrella. They encourage learner involvement and group activity. These models do not encourage much individual activity nor one-to-one relationships because the plenary session or working group will be the focus for most of the learning.

Our alternative models have characteristics which make them suitable for different situations. Learners may feel they are challenged by the new possibilities and opt for an exciting, new approach to learning. Their choice should be made in the knowledge that the model chosen will provide a viable alternative for success.

Situations where the learner and the content are suited to one-to-one learning relationships may lead to contracts or tutorial models. These models do have limitations which should be considered.

The covenant or contract (see chapter 12) works best with advanced levels of content in a situation where the learner is highly motivated and competent. It should be used in situations where the learner requires a plan in order to provide security or where the content is of sufficient complexity to make it necessary to follow a plan to insure success.

The tutorial (see chapter 13) provides a close working relationship which provides considerable benefit to the learner. It can be an alternative to the one-to-one situation of the covenant when the learner does not wish to have a plan to follow. Flexibility is more likely to be available to the learner under this model.

Both previously described alternative models stress one-to-one situations which will be helpful to persons in isolated learning situations. There is a price to pay, however, for this one-to-one situation. That price involves the lack of community involvement and the resultant isolation which may not be desirable. Other models enable community as well as learning.

Tough's model (see chapter 14) enables individual learning within a group context. This model combines structured and nonstructured components which satisfy those who seek both options. The structure is in the class sessions which follow the andragogical model in part. The other activities stress support for individual learning and an expansive approach to growth and development.

Griffin's model (see chapter 15) provides a solid group context for growth and development. This model will appeal to those who enjoy working in sub-groups. Advanced material is best for this model because group direction and input can be done best with prior background in an area. The major value of this model, in my opinion, is the way it supports the learning transition to self-direction.

The Scandinavian Study Circle (see chapter 16) involves a democratic group process for decision making and shared responsibility for learning. Here we move from the individual focus of previous chapters to a model which will emphasize the value of the group. This does not mean that individual rights and interests are not respected. It is more a question of emphasis on the need for the community to work together effectively to assist in the achievement of both community and individual goals. Obviously, this is a model to be utilized when priority is placed upon the group and the building of community.

Paulo Freire has provided us with another model for building community and for learning and growing together (see chapter 17). This prominent educator challenges us to work with the groups in our community which need to learn together to achieve justice and fairness in society. The group's learning is the clear focus for this model.

There is one more model for group learning which is presented in this volume. Action research (see chapter 18) provides a basis for a group to gain new knowledge, skills, and attitudes for community action. The research component involves the discovery of whatever is required to take community action. The action component is the intended result of the learning, but the process of learning may shape the action component.

When learners do not have ready access to each other, human and material resources, meeting places, or face-to-face facilitation on a regular basis we need to consider the distance approach to learning (see chapter 19). Distance education will provide the opportunities for learning for those persons who live in remote areas or who lack ready access to resources through personal circumstances.

The models are displayed with ratings in relation to each of three domains in the chart in this chapter. Some words of explanation may help the reader to understand the particular ratings which have occurred.

The reader should remember that these models have been developed in most cases without thought for a particular domain. They have evolved from practice and have been refined through analysis and practice. I suspect that Freire's term, "praxis,"[15] would be an appropriate way to describe how many models develop. The result of this process of development is that we may suggest that a model is appropriate for a particular domain without limiting it to that suggestion.

The following chart sees models as having certain strengths. My view is that one might utilize models where a Good to Excellent rating is indicated in preference to those which are merely rated Average. The fact that models may be "mixing" the domains should be taken into account when making the decision.

Chart 1: Models Rated According to Taxonomy of Content

MODEL\CONTENT	KNOWLEDGE	ATTITUDE	LIFESTYLE
Andragogical	Good	Good	Good
Inter-generational	Good	Good	Very Good
Independent	Good	Good	Good
Covenant	Good	Poor	Average
Nondirective	Good	Good	Good
Tip of Iceberg	Very Good	Good	Good
Interdependent	Good	Excellent	Good
Study Circle	Good	Good	Very Good
Freirien	Good	Good	Very Good
Action	Good	Average	Very Good
Distance	Good	Poor	Average

SUMMARY

Choose the model which is right for the learner, the content, the context, and you. Recognize the needs, interests, and values of the learner in order to insure that the program will work. Determine the best way the content can be learned. Consider the context for both its possibilities and its limitations. Remember your own strengths and weaknesses and your reactions to models as you prepare to choose. Each model has its place in the spectrum of options, but each situation requires careful thought before the final choice is made.

Notes

1. *Webster's New Collegiate Dictionary* (Springfield, Mass.: G.&C. Merriam, 1976), p. 1209.

2. Thomas H. Groome, *Christian Religious Education: Sharing our Story and Vision* (San Francisco: Harper & Row, 1980), pp. 175-177.

3. Malcolm S. Knowles, *The Modern Practice of Adult Education: From Pedagogy to Andragogy* (Chicago: Follett, 1980), pp. 43-44.

4. Ibid., pp. 51-52.

5. Malcolm S. Knowles, *Self-Directed Learning: A Guide for Learners and Teachers* (New York: Association Press, 1975), and *Using Learning Contracts* (San Francisco: Jossey-Bass, 1986), pp. 6-8.

6. Stephen D. Brookfield, *Understanding and Facilitating Adult Learning* (San Francisco: Jossey-Bass, 1986), p. 41.

7. L.S. Guglielmino, Development of the Self-Directed Learning Readiness Scale (Doctoral dissertation, Department of Adult Education, The University of Georgia, 1977).

8. Benjamin S. Bloom, ed., *The Taxonomy of Educational Objectives: The Classification of Educational Goals: Handbook 1* (New York: David McKay, 1969).

9. James Michael Lee, *The Content of Religious Instruction: A Social Science Approach* (Birmingham, Ala.: Religious Education Press, 1985).

10. Ibid., p. 13.

11. Ibid., p. 14.

12. Ibid.

13. Ibid., p. 15.

14. Nancy T. Foltz, "Basic Principles of Adult Religious Education," in *Handbook of Adult Religious Education*, ed. Nancy T. Foltz (Birmingham, Ala.: Religious Education Press, 1986), p. 26.

15. Paulo Freire, *Pedagogy of the Oppressed* (New York: Seabury, 1970), pp. 75-76.

Chapter 6

The Traditional Or Andragogical Model In The Context Of Religious Education

The most commonly recognized model of adult education within the religious education context or any other context is the andragogical model described by Malcolm Knowles. This author, professor, and practitioner did much to popularize the effective model in his books. His best known volume, *The Modern Practice of Adult Education: From Pedagogy to Andragogy*, provides us with an excellent review of this model from a general adult education perspective.[1]

Knowles correctly pays tribute to the Europeans for their involvement in the development of the concept of andragogy.[2] Reference is made in an earlier volume, *The Modern Practice of Adult Education: Pedagogy versus Andragogy*,[3] to the article by Dusan Savicevic in the first issue of the journal, *Convergence*,[4] but this reference is missing from the previously cited revised edition. In *The Adult Learner: A Neglected Species*, Knowles also acknowledges his debt to the Yugoslavians for the term which defined this new approach.[5]

Authors such as Leon McKenzie[6] and Nancy Foltz[7] have described the andragogical model quite favorably in relation to the practice of adult religious education. It is a model which has permeated adult religious education because of its pragmatic, effective approach, but like all models it could benefit from some reexamination and up-dating.

John Elias reminds us of the important role adult religious education plays in the affective domain in his volume, *The Foundations and Practice of Adult Religious Education*.[8] He states that it is important "to maximize the

45

positive attitudes and emotions of the adult learner while minimizing the negative attitudes and barriers."[9] This model sets a standard for the affective domain which should be met by the other models.

One of the reasons why this model is successful is that it recognizes certain key characteristics of adult learners. Many alternative models developed since the 1960s include certain positive components of this traditional mode. Other alternative models such as the Study Circle appear to incorporate features of the andragogical model in spite of their separate development. Those practitioners who would prefer to use alternative models should review this model because they will gain insight into activities such as climate setting, active learning, and the learner evaluation of the program.

An important component of the model is seen in its adaptation of the program development model for the schools curricula to the adult setting. When Knowles used the phrase, "from pedagogy to andragogy," in the title of his book he was reflecting, in part, the transition one needs to make from the school to the adult program. His title for the first edition, *The Modern Practice of Adult Education: Pedagogy versus Andragogy*, puts an even greater emphasis on the need to make a transition.

The change in titles between the two books reflects both a change in the thinking of Knowles and in the thinking of other adult educators between the 1960s and the 1980s. The changes in education which occurred in the intervening period made adult educators feel more accepting of their colleagues in primary and secondary education. Perhaps adult educators also felt less defensive about their field and no longer needed to defend it by emphasizing differences.

WHAT IS ANDRAGOGY?

The principles upon which the andragogical model is based stress the amount of prior experience adults bring to the learning situation, the mature self-concept of adults, the readiness to learn certain tasks, and the orientation to learning which looks to immediate application and problem centeredness. The following figure contains excerpts from Knowles' description of the pedagogical and andragogical models. I have enclosed the comments on andragogy only:

Figure 1

1. It is a normal aspect of the process of human development to move from dependency toward increasing self-directedness, but at different rates for different people and in different dimensions of life. Teachers have a responsibility to encourage and nurture this movement. Adults have a deep psychological need to be generally self-directing, although they may be dependent in particular temporary situations.

2. As people grow and develop they accumulate an increasing reservoir of experience that becomes an increasingly rich resource for learning—for themselves and for others. Furthermore, people attach more meaning to learnings
they gain from experience than those they acquire passively. Accordingly
some primary facilitational techniques in adult education include experiential
techniques—laboratory experiments, discussion, problem solving, case studies, simulation exercises, field experience, and the like.

3. People become ready to learn something when they experience a need to
learn it in order to cope more satisfyingly with real-life tasks or problems.
The educator has responsibility to create conditions and provide tools and
procedures for helping learners discover their "need to know." Learning programs should be organized around life-application categories and sequenced
according to learners' readiness to learn.

4. Learners see education as a process of developing increased competence to
achieve their full potential in life. They want to be able to apply whatever
knowledge and skill they gain today to living more effectively tomorrow.
Accordingly, learning experiences should be organized around competency-
development categories. People are performance-centered in their orientation to learning.[10]

The practical applications of these principles must be considered before we
determine their application in the adult religious education setting.

It is clear that adults need to consider their prior experience as they learn
because integration will enhance learning. Adults filter new information,
experiences, and feelings through the memory bank of prior experience.

May I suggest an illustration of this principle in the way in which you
read this book? You will read a chapter with a view to its application in
familiar situations. What makes sense to you will be retained and integrated
into your approach to adult religious education. What does not pass through
this filter of knowledge and experience will be rejected because it will be seen
as inappropriate or inapplicable.

It is impossible to separate adults from the wealth of experience they
bring to the learning situation. Rather than attempt to deny or discount this
experience, educators should attempt to benefit from it and to assist the
learner to utilize it.

A difficulty may arise from a situation in which the learner has learned
something previously either formally or informally which does not have a continuing validity. This may hamper new learning, but it need not be an insurmountable problem. If you plan to take into account previous learning which is
no longer helpful or appropriate, the adjustments can be made subject to your
ability to demonstrate to the learner the validity of the new knowledge, attitude, or skill as opposed to the formerly acquired knowledge, attitude, or skill.

Another assumption of andragogy is that the growth process by which
adults are differentiated from children leads to a desire for responsibility.

If an adult has responsibility for decision making in other areas of life, why should that sense of responsibility not be carried over into the educational or learning area of life? The response is that the adult is likely to wish to gain control over those things which can be controlled.

This issue of self-control or direction is somewhat problematic for many adults. Their experience of classrooms has normally been "other" directed. They have expectations of classrooms based on this earlier experience and they are willing to forego self-direction at times in order to gain something new. The fact that it happens does not always make it the best or most sought after situation for mature adults.

This model does permit learner contributions to the process of planning and delivering workshops, seminars, courses, etc. It does not build the effective process of transition to learner control which is found in other models.

Another assumption of andragogy is drawn from Robert Havighurst and his concept of the developmental tasks through the life span.[11] Knowles clearly regards this research as indicative of a valid pattern of adult development which will enable the educator to predict areas of learning needs.

A further comment by Havighurst indicates that, not only can success be predicted, but the teacher will find the learner to be most receptive to the teaching process.[12] Knowles takes this comment on the "teachable moment" further to reflect the learner's perspective when he states that the learner will experience a state of "readiness to learn" when engaged in accomplishing the developmental tasks.[13]

The one difficulty we may have in this process may be found in the application by Knowles of the developmental task concept. If we agree with the concept, we shall need to up-date developmental tasks based quite clearly on the socio-cultural context. If we do not subscribe to the developmental task concept, the meaning for this assumption may be found in the fact that adults do feel the need to learn certain things at certain times in their lives. There is simply another explanation for why this need exists.

Knowles also refers to adult learners as having an orientation to learning which is "performance-centered."[14] They wish to be able to achieve their potential and to solve problems which may block this achievement.

My view of this situation is that adult learners are rooted in life. There is a connection between the learning aspect and the other aspects of their lives. This is the essence of the holistic approach to education.

Why I state that the andragogical model is like the traditional school model is that it retains the basic components of need identification, purposes and objectives, program design, and evaluation. It correctly attempts to adapt these components to the adult learner and the new setting of adult education institutions.

The process of adaptation via andragogical principles often involves a softening of the objectives to insure flexibility. This flexibility is needed to insure that the needs of the learners who actually participate in an event are met. The need identification process which occurs with a select group prior to an event often has limited success in predicting the precise needs which must be translated into educational objectives. This is true because the learners who actually participate in an event may include many who were not part of the prior procedure.

The principles of andragogy were described initially by Knowles in relation to the learning activities of groups. *The Modern Practice of Adult Education*[15] reviews these assumptions as a prelude to the methods and techniques of adult education for both large and small group settings. It should be noted that his later work in learning contracts also applies the assumptions in the context of an alternative model.

The perception of adult educators in the 1950s when Knowles was in the formative stages of his career and when he was considering and developing these assumptions was that groups should be the focus of their attention. The major study of adult learning activities in the United States performed by Johnstone and Rivera outlines the participation of adults in educational groups.[16] Their views, as outlined in the book, may be seen as typical of most adult educators until the writings of such visionaries as C.O. Houle and Allen Tough began to influence our thinking.

Both John Elias[17] and Stephen Brookfield[18] have commented on the limitations of the andragogical model. Elias admits that Knowles has identified certain important characteristics which are important to the adult religious educator, but it is clear that the concept of lifelong learning is more important to him.[19]

Elias' concerns about andragogy are related to the lack of research which exists in relation to the model and to the differentiation between pedagogy and andragogy.[20] Perhaps good andragogy is good pedagogy for many educators like Elias.

One weakness of the andragogical model is based in the very fact that it does not move sufficiently away from the traditional school-based approach to curriculum. It is simply a more agreeable form of schooling for adults. This will not be acceptable to many adults who seek real alternatives to a school-based approach to learning.

There are assumptions behind the andragogical model based upon the cultural context from which it emerged. In certain respects, the andragogical model may be making assumptions about how adults should be rather than how they are. As we have seen earlier in this chapter, Knowles suggests that independence emerges as a key aspect of the mature adult. The difficulty with this statement is that it applies to that large group of adults who tend to participate in adult education activities, the middle class. It does not take into account the factors which derive from other cultural backgrounds.

Elias[21] indicates quite correctly that the aging process is a factor here in relation to older adulthood. The changes in the developmental processes of older adulthood may lead to a decreased sense of independence. Although it is true that many older adults will experience this change, I believe that we should consider many older adults as quite capable of maintaining independence while they maintain physical and mental health.

The most important weakness of the andragogical model in the view of this author is in its interpretation of developmental tasks and other "needs" as sufficient to define the goals and objectives for learning. It is an instrumental attitude which allows us to interpret the needs of students in this way.

ANDRAGOGY AND ADULT RELIGIOUS EDUCATION

What do these thoughts contribute to our understanding of religious education for adults? I believe that there is much to be considered in each one. The concepts of self-direction, experience, readiness to learn, and life centeredness are important to adult religious educators for unique reasons.

Although the adult learner may seek guidance from time to time from a religious advisor, he or she must be satisfied in the final analysis with the results of the growth which occurs. Adults will engage in other-directed programs on occasion and be rewarded for their efforts. There will also be times when they wish to act individually or under their own direction. We need to recognize both needs.

We must never deny, of course, the value of individual religious experience. It is a part of reality to affirm that each person will experience the presence of "something or someone beyond the self" in some way. I suggest that we should affirm and support this experience.

Anyone who has worked with adults in a variety of settings will recognize both moments of curiosity and of anxiety to know. It is within these moments that we can begin to open the way to learning. Research demonstrates that personal growth will often happen as the result of adverse circumstances.[22]

I do not fully agree with the last assumption as stated by Knowles but I do see the need for our work to be related to the life of the learner. If we become esoteric and distant from our learners and do not consider their circumstances, we shall be considered irrelevant by them.

THE UTILIZATION OF THE TRADITIONAL MODEL

Many adults feel quite comfortable with the traditional adult education model which allows for the input of information and the process of discussion and integration. Those adults who are comfortable with a model which combines the strengths of the familiar pedagogical model with a recognition of the nature of adulthood will appreciate this approach.

The model should be used with those adults who are comfortable with it and able to learn successfully within its confines. Adults who like both groups and a more traditional plan will attend those groups which involve courses that conform to the andragogical model.

The flexibility of this model allows it to be used with both large and small groups. The learning process may flow back and forth between the larger and smaller groups if this is desirable. The nominal group activity can be introduced to incorporate an individual component to the process part of the time.

Please note that this is a model which, by its very nature, places more emphasis on learning within the group than as an individual. It is not a model, however, which should be utilized if one's aim is social change. It does not have the strengths of other models which were developed for these very specific purposes. The model should be used for the strengths it does possess.

The specific suggestions for programs and courses based upon this model will be found in the following chapters on program planning and evaluation. The principles of andragogy are implicit also in the chapter on Learning Contracts which also comes from an alternative model by Knowles

Notes

1. Malcolm S. Knowles, *The Modern Practice of Adult Education: From Pedagogy to Andragogy* (Revised and Updated)(Chicago: Follett, 1980).

2. Ibid., p. 42.

3. Malcolm S. Knowles, *The Modern Practice of Adult Education: Pedagogy versus Andragogy* (Houston: Gulf Publishing, 1970), p. 38.

4. Dusan Savicevic, "Training Adult Educationists in Yugoslavia," *Convergence* 1, no. 1 (March, 1968), pp. 69-75.

5. Malcolm S. Knowles, *The Adult Learner: A Neglected Species* (Houston: Gulf Publishing, 1973), p. 40.

6. Leon McKenzie, *The Religious Education of Adults* (Birmingham, Ala.: Religious Education Press, 1982), pp. 120-125.

7. Nancy T. Foltz, "Basic Principals of Adult Religious Education," in *Handbook of Adult Religious Education*, ed. Nancy T. Foltz (Birmingham, Ala.: Religious Education Press, 1986), pp. 30 and 31.

8. John L. Elias, *The Foundations and Practice of Adult Religious Education* (Malabar, Fla.: Kreiger, 1982), p. 103.

9. Ibid.

10. Ibid., pp. 43 and 44.

11. Robert J. Havighurst, *Developmental Tasks and Education* (New York: David McKay, 1961) and Knowles, *The Modern Practice of Adult Education: From Pedagogy to Andragogy*, pp. 51-52.

12. Havighurst, *Developmental Tasks and Education*, p. 5.

13. Knowles, *The Modern Practice of Adult Education: From Pedagogy to Andragogy*, p. 51.

14. Ibid., p. 44.

15. Ibid., pp. 40-54.

16. William Johnstone and R. J. Rivera, *Volunteers for Learning* (Chicago: Aldine Publishing, 1965), p. XXV.

17. Elias, T*he Foundations and Practice of Adult Religious Education*, pp. 114-116.

18. Stephen D. Brookfield, *Understanding and Facilitating Adult Learning* (San Francisco: Jossey-Bass, 1986), pp. 95-101.

19. Elias, *The Foundations and Practice of Adult Religious Education*, pp. 115-116.

20. John L. Elias, "Andragogy Revisited," *Adult Education* 29: 4 (Summer, 1979), p. 255.

21. Ibid., p. 115.

22. R.E.Y. Wickett, "Adult Learning and Spiritual Growth," *Religious Education* 75: 5 (July-August, 1980), pp. 452-461.

Chapter 7

Program Planning
And Implementation
In Adult Religious Education

The Andragogical Model provides us with a versatile, proven approach to the education of adults in general and the religious education of adults in particular. The successes of this model are well documented in the literature of the field. It will work effectively with a significant number of adults in a wide range of content areas.

The roots of this model are to be found in the traditional educational program planning model of Ralph Tyler[1] and the adaptation by Malcolm Knowles[2] of this model to the adult context. The secret to the success of the model is the way it adapts to the adult situation without losing the structural strengths of the planning process.

The major strength of the model exists in its ability to provide an organizational structure within which the facilitator and the learner can plan their activities. This organizational structure takes into account the requirements of both parties to the learning interaction.

Facilitators and learners frequently wish to know where they are proceeding with the learning process. A guide or plan which provides the basis for continuing activity must take certain factors into account. Perhaps the most critical factor is the requirement that learners' needs and interests be taken into account in any program. Additional requirements, such as the appropriateness of activities to content, can be incorporated also into a planning process.

The major feature of this model can be seen in its objectification of the learning. The essential element of the process is that the learning can be based upon goals and objectives toward which the learner strives.[3] We must organize our learning in relation to the end product. The achievement of the goals and objectives assumes immense importance in this model.

Tyler's model for the development of the goals and objectives involved the examination of the learners,[4] of contemporary life external to the school,[5] plus content specialists' ideas.[6] These ideas were then interpreted in the light of the philosophical and psychological principles of learning which were prevalent at the time. Tyler describes the process as a form of screening.[7]

The final part of the process involves formulating the objectives in a manner which is appropriate to aid the teaching and learning process. This will enable the planner to select the requisite learning experiences for the learners and to organize these experiences in an effective manner. Evaluative procedures are to be made consistent with the plans.

Tyler has three important criteria which are to be utilized in the organization of learning activities. These criteria include continuity, sequence, and integration.[8] The principles of andragogy would suggest that the latter criterion would be important because of the wealth of experience adults bring to the learning situation.

There is one important aspect to Tyler's model which endears it to many educators and that is its evaluative capacity. This model provides a clear basis for the evaluation of the students' learning based upon their ability to demonstrate the achievement of objectives.

Perhaps this is an aspect which does not endear it to many adult learners who, for the most part, do not wish their performance to be evaluated externally. The manner in which Knowles and many of his colleagues in the field of adult education have chosen to respond to this adult reaction is to avoid student evaluation. Knowles advocates the use of objectives and other parts of the Tyler model but indicates a preference for program evaluation as opposed to student evaluation in most situations. The absence of suggestions for student performance evaluation in *The Modern Practice of Adult Education* supports this point of view.[9]

This poses a very important problem for those who would seek "hard data" to confirm the effectiveness of an adult education model. We tend to rely on the anecdotal data or other measures of success which are frequently less than ideal. One does find it difficult to accept the model on this basis, but the widespread, continuing use of the model does provide some basis for our inclusion of it in this book.

I suggest that those adult religious educators who choose to use this model should consider the ways in which Knowles has adapted it to conform to adult requirements. Knowles sees learner input into the process as valuable during the program at appropriate intervals.[10] He cites Daniel Stufflebeam's Formative or "decision-making" evaluation as a valuable part of the planning process.[11]

METHODOLOGY

Malcolm Knowles has provided us with a valuable list of decision points and components for the andragogical process. The following list provides us with clear reference points:

1. A possible educational activity is identified.
2. A decision is made to proceed.
3. Objectives are identified and refined.
4. A suitable format is designed.
5. The format is fitted into larger patterns of life.
6. The plan is put into effect.
7. The results are measured and appraised.[12]

A further description of numbers four and five may be useful. Number four would include consideration of "resources, leaders, methods, schedule, sequence, social reinforcement, individualization, roles and relationships, criteria of evaluation, and clarity of design" according to Knowles.[13] A critical part of number five involves the financing of the program.

This model begins with an idea for a course. The sources of the idea may be varied but the end result is the course, program, or some such entity. The nature of the program will vary from a major conference to a small group meeting, but the initial idea is critical to its later development.

The ideas which appear to be the most successful are often ideas that emerge from some group or community, but the possibility of an individual's bright idea should be considered. I would caution you to consider the response of others to the idea before proceeding. Listen carefully without being carried too far forward in what may prove to be individual enthusiasm and lead to a negative result in registrations.

The next stage should involve a planning committee or group[14] to refine the idea and to help operationalize it. This committee should be composed of interested parties. Its size will depend upon the nature of the proposed program with a carefully selected membership (where reality permits). It is important to have enough people to do the necessary tasks as well as to add to the creative atmosphere. Edgar Boone talks about the ways of identifying and involving leaders who can assist in this process of program formation through some group process.[15]

The most important task involves the organization of the learning process for the future group of learners. This follows the systematic approach of need identification, objective setting, planning the learning activities, and evaluation procedures. This will be followed by an organizational process which will enable us to operationalize the program for its potential learners.

Figure A

**PLANNING PROCESS
(Adapted from Kowles)**

Educational Activity Identified	Formal Decision to Proceed	Specific Needs Identified	Objectives Clearly Stated	Format Designed	Format Put in Context	Implementation	Evaluation

The andragogical model relies heavily upon the existence of some form of identifiable "need" which can be used as the base for a program. We can use a variety of methods to collect information about these forces including verbal and written, face-to-face or at a distance, and dialogue or monologue. We can collect the information from "experts," prospective learners, or other interested parties. Questionnaires, interviews, or discussion groups will enable us to gain information to be utilized in the planning process.

The best process should involve using more than one available and appropriate method for need identification. I prefer the methods which involve face-to-face discussions with as many persons as possible, but the alternatives exist to enable us to gather information where face-to-face methods will produce insufficient information.

It is my contention that the information collected may take several forms including that which goes beyond the content of the learning. Preferred arrangements for time, physical arrangements, and location may be communicated and received during this process. The program may be great, but the wrong timing or place can have a serious negative impact.

I also have a strong personal preference for involving people in the process. Wherever possible, this means forming a planning committee who will help to perform the tasks and utilizing interviews or group discussion to collect information. I suggest this because the information gathered tends to be better and clearer *and* because the commitment to participate is built through such involvement. If you don't want people to come, use your own idea and plan without reference to anyone else. If you do want people to come, arrange for involvement at the first opportunity and continue to have people involved throughout the process.

Committees should be representative without being cumbersome. They need to have the information which comes from a serious review of the situation in order to avoid the limitations of personal prejudice. The committee should see itself as having interests beyond the small group.

Some groups will be attracted to the concept of need as a gap, or the distance between the desired level of knowledge or skill or attitude and the present level. Others will want to examine more complex theories which make reference to sociological and psychological theories. In either situation, the ability to identify specifics will be helpful in this model.

One danger which arises from the high profile of education and the attempts of some educators to "sell" education as a panacea is that people want education to solve all problems. In reality, the educational process is not a panacea but a tool which should be used selectively and appropriately. By itself, education will not transform your faith community nor will it change personal situations. What it can do is to assist the process of change.

The planning committee should make a distinction between changes which will occur through the accretion of new knowledge, skills, or attitudes and those which require other action. Not all needs will be met by education alone.

The next step involves the translation of the "need" into the purpose and objectives which will identify and shape the program. This is a critical step because so many other aspects of the program depend upon it. This model requires the setting of "targets" which are to be sought in the learning process.

The identification of reasonable objectives will give the potential learner a sense of where the course is headed and establish a basis for decisions about registration and participation. They will provide resource persons with the necessary information to enable preparations. Evaluation should stem from objectives in this model also.

"Activity" objectives may be more critical to the andragogical model than the "behavioral" objectives of the Tyler model. The difference is that an activity is described by the former while a result is described by the latter. The following examples may assist the reader to understand the difference:

EXAMPLE 1:
The behavioral objective may be stated as "the learner will be able to identify the books of the New Testament."

EXAMPLE 2:
The activity objective may be stated as "the group will review the Book of John with reference to its unique role among the gospels."

This will enable the learner in a noncredit situation to identify the specific results he wishes to achieve while guaranteeing the content area which will be the subject of the program. I prefer to allow the learners to identify, wherever possible, the specific results of the learning for themselves.

There may be times when quite specific behavioral objectives are useful to a program. If the program involves training in a particular skill for ministry or in some area where it is desirable for planners, resource persons, and learners to have specific objectives, please do utilize them. I do not disagree with the use of behavioral objectives, only to their overuse with adults.

The appropriate program must be based upon the objective, or objectives, which have been identified as appropriate for the learners. Resource persons with a good knowledge of both the content area and process requirements should be engaged at an early stage. Interaction with the planning committee will produce positive results in many instances. These content and process specialists should be able to guide the overall planning.

The pattern followed most often in these circumstances is to describe the needs and objectives to the resource person or persons so that they understand the requirements for content and process. These resource persons are able to plan to meet these requirements.

I find it useful to either review the plans of the resource persons myself as planner or to have the committee do so. The latter approach is the most useful in my opinion. It is more difficult for the resource person to force an opinion on a good committee than on an individual planner.

Physical facilities are very important to virtually all programs. Accessibility and reasonable comfort will insure continued attendance. Location is a factor, particularly in urban settings where safety may be a factor. As a resident of an area with a harsh winter climate, I am aware that people want to leave early when the wind and snow threaten.

Physical arrangements for seating of plenary and sub-group meetings should be planned carefully. The details from washrooms to parking need to be a part of the overall planning process. The following list includes items which I find useful to remember:

1. Convenient location of meeting rooms to entrances, and so on.
2. Convenient location of rooms to each other, if required.
3. Appropriate seating, not too comfortable but reasonable.
4. Convenient transportation, accessible to public and private means of transportation.
5. Good sight lines for speakers, video displays, etc.
6. Good audio facilities, microphones where needed.
7. Appropriate variety of food and drink services (coffee plus).
8. Convenient and appropriate accommodations as required.[16]

I believe that the completion of the physical part of the arrangements will enable the learning component to proceed with fewer interruptions.

The organization of the "registration" procedures should maximize the positive perception of a welcome environment for the course. If people have problems obtaining information about the event or in joining the group, they may choose another activity instead. A name and telephone number on information sheets, posters, or brochures will facilitate contact. Convenient hours for information and registration by mail are often used to assist the potential learner to interact with program organizers.

The program should contain a variety of opportunities for learning, depending upon the nature of the objectives. The following points describe factors to be considered in the program to be delivered:

1. Hospitable and comfortable learning climate.
2. Introductions which build relationships with all parties.
3. Review of prior knowledge, skill, attitudes as needed.
4. Introduction of new knowledge, skills, attitudes as needed.
5. Integration process for new and prior knowledge, etc.

Each of these points must be considered in relation to the individual and the group situation.

Climate Setting

Knowles defines the characteristics of a climate which is conducive to learning as including both physiological and psychological elements.[17] Accordingly, Knowles suggests that the critical experience of the learners at the beginning of a learning process can inhibit or create the appropriate situation for productivity during the remainder of the time spent.[18]

There are several factors to consider in the process, but the most important for me involves the recognition of the nature of the group. The exercises or activities should always be appropriate for the group.

The second factor which should be considered is the process of learning which will follow the opening session. It is always valuable, wherever possible, to make the climate-setting activity lead into the activities which are to follow.

Some practical activities include having persons introduce themselves orally or in written or picture form to another individual, sub-group, or plenary. Variations on the theme can occur by having people introduce themselves to one person who will then introduce them to others.

When the group is experienced with learning situations, it is possible to seek wider communication, such as the introduction of someone else to the rest of the group (groups of twenty or less). In a larger group or situations where people are less experienced and shy the individual or sub-group situation to enable more comfortable introductions should be used.

If the group members are seated at tables with four to six persons, talking will have begun before the session opens. This will be a most convenient situation for climate setting for shy persons.

Some situations will include the opportunity to use written comments for introductions. I frequently ask students to provide a few statements along with their name on a five-by-seven card. They show this to another person and then chat about themselves for a few moments. When the discussions are over (sometimes after they have met four or five people in this way), I collect the cards for future reference during the course.

EXAMPLE 1

Reg. Wickett

1. University professor
2. Lay reader
3. Husband and father
4. Likes tennis and "old-timers" hockey

Another use I have for the cards involves the time when I wish students to express themselves in picture format. I suggest that they write their first name in the middle and draw a simple picture in each corner or quadrant of the card to represent themselves. This approach works very well when I want them to use other parts of their mind as well as the traditional intellectual part.

Example 2:

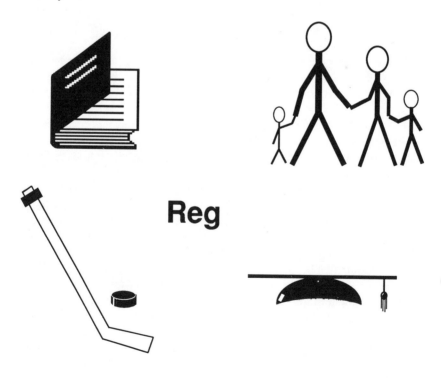

Reg

The first two points reflect the need for a secure learning environment which is true for most adults. Although I can accept the fact that some adults do learn under stress or in a hostile situation, I believe that the majority of adults will learn best under conditions which are supportive and comfortable most of the time.

Knowles does indicate in the assumptions of andragogy that adults bring prior experience to the learning situation.[19] The opportunity to recall and examine the prior experience may determine the success or failure of the new learning. This is often the case because learners cannot integrate if they have not prepared for the integration process.

Some programs will need to incorporate new and prior learning into an integrated whole. Some programs will need to add to existing knowledge or skill. Another program may need to help learners "unlearn" or discard something which is no longer relevant.

Adults will integrate the new learning and discard old learning when they are convinced of the merit of such action. An examination of existing knowledge, skills, and attitudes will help convince learners of the merits as well as to make it possible to integrate.

One critical area for decision making involves the various methods for teaching which will be chosen to support the learning process. The following points may be useful for consideration of the most appropriate choices.

1. The resource person must feel reasonably comfortable with the choices.
2. The teaching method should fit the objective(s).
3. The learners must accept the method as appropriate.
4. Variety and ability to stimulate should be considered.
5. Time for thought and integration should be included, especially in situations where attitudinal changes are involved.

It is difficult in a short chapter to mention and comment on all methods. The short statements which follow will provide some general guidelines to assist the reader.

Groups and their Utilization

Group discussions create relationships which enable both individual and group learning to meet objectives. One of the best sources for this area is the book, *Joining Together*, by Johnson and Johnson.[20] *Groups: Leadership and Group Development* by Hedley Dimock is also a useful volume.[21] Define the task and process clearly for the group at the beginning and do not be afraid to provide notes for group members or discussion leaders.

Consider the approach of James White when he refers to the importance of self-worth or self-esteem to the person and to the group. White cites the well-known author, Virginia Satir, as an authority for this position.[22] Satir also is concerned with intergenerational relationships and learning from the point of view of the family counselor.

White goes on further to comment on the impact of questioning, again citing Satir on this point. When questions are asked of people in a group or family, it enhances their feelings of self-worth.[23] I agree that questioning will have both a positive effect upon the individual to whom the question is asked as well as often providing a source for information for the facilitator and others.

The following steps to learning represent the process by which many groups can engage in a satisfactory way to complete the learning process. The steps were designed to illustrate the way in which the process may be undertaken. I suggest it as one option rather than a prescription for all learning processes.

Steps to Learning in Groups

1. Discover: the process by which something new is revealed whether it is new information, skill, or any other thing to be learned.

2. Examine: the process by which one examines or considers the new information, and so on, which has been discovered.

3. Share: the process which involves sharing one's own results of discovery and examination and hearing the results of either one other's discovery and examination or that of a group of others.

4. Analysis: the process by which the group continues the process of examination which emerges from the sharing process in order to enable the learners to deepen their understanding through a collective process.

5. Decision: the process by which the learners determine how to apply that which has been learned. This may be done individually or collectively, but some sharing will reinforce individual decisions.

6. Action: the process of putting into action the decisions learners have made.

7. Reaction: the process by which the learning continues after the event as new data are generated by action.

Further explanation of each step may assist the reader to understand how the process will occur.

I believe that all learning experiences have an element of something new. This "new" aspect may be seen as somewhat special or it may be "a matter of course," so to speak. Whether it is exciting or not, the learner will need to accept the new item which is perceived.

The requirement to examine the experience more closely in order to obtain all that it contains is what the next step is about. It may be slightly difficult if there is too much excitement in a discovery. Learners do find it to be helpful in all but the most limited discoveries.

The sharing process is natural to some but not to all. It is here that our discovery will be better remembered and understood. The activity of discussion and the reinforcement of memory through repetition will assist the learning process.

A group discussion of shared and different experiences will reinforce and expand the reservoir of experience on which the analysis will be performed. The analysis enables time for thought and depth of understanding. There are limitations upon the things people can do individually. This has the capacity to enhance learning even when the experiences have been individual and separate.

Perhaps the most difficult part of the process is to determine what meaning the learning has for the future. The frustration that may result for some forms of learning if this activity does not occur could be considerable. Some forms of learning will, in fact, demand further steps.

There is also the fact that most learning does affect us in some way. The idea behind this process is to control and direct the learning in ways that will be most meaningful for each person.

The action phase may require reinforcement and support. This may be built into the decision-making phase. Learning partners and groups will reinforce the action phase in many instances.

If there is no action, the entire learning process may be seen as incomplete by some learners. The enjoyment of learning in and of itself may not be enough for many learners. If the purpose of learning is to be able to do something such as perform a service in ministry, one can see the relevance. Should one be seeking understanding, the relevance may be just as important because of the potential impact of understanding on future actions and life experiences.

There will be a new set of data generated by our actions. This will recommence the process of learning all over again, should we choose to do so.

These steps owe much to my consideration over the years of the writings of several authors; including Dewey, Lewin, Freire, and particularly Kolb.[24] These authors introduced me to the process of steps or stages to describe this particular type of situation.

It is important to insure that the group is the appropriate size and has the required resources for the task to be performed. The ideal learning group is competent, but it should also be committed. A recognition of the value of externally created goals or a set of goals developed by the group will insure the latter, as well in the inclusion of appropriate levels of knowledge, skill, etc.

The use of simulated experiences in the form of games or role playing can be a powerful way of assisting people to learn. A very fine description of the process from the educator's perspective may be seen in Joyce and Weil's chapter, "Learning from Simulation," in their book on models.[25]

The four phases of the process are "orientation, participant training, the simulation itself, and the debriefing."[26] The simulation game will require the most preparation, but the role playing situations in shorter experiences should include all four phases also.

The debriefing phase enables one to draw the relevant learning from the experience. Please note that feelings are often critical to the simulation experience. They can not be ignored in the debriefing phase.

Attitudes and values can be examined in this way, but people can test their interactive, personal skills through simulations. I have seen simulations used effectively to help learners understand the complexity of racial and other situations. They have been employed also to assist in the development of interviewing techniques and other interpersonal skills.

A variety of other methods, both old and new, can be used quite appropriately within the context of the andragogical model. Books and other publications which describe the methods should be consulted where necessary. The question to be asked about the use of any method in this context of andragogy is, "Does this method conform to the four basic assumptions?" If the answer is in the affirmative, proceed with usage.

SUMMARY

The andragogical model is a successful, pragmatic approach to the delivery of programs for adults. It will work in the religious education context with adults who want to participate in a traditional model which recognizes their adulthood. It should be considered for use with a variety of educational objectives including cognitive skills and attitudinal objectives.

The weaknesses of this model lie in the fact that it is essentially a didactic, school-based model with its clear objectification of learning. Perhaps many learners will find the similarity to school-based learning too inappropriate for their needs. I suggest that this model will clearly be less helpful with those persons who reject the style of education thus implied because of prior negative experiences.

The issue of "objectification" may also be a matter to be considered carefully. Does the search for religious development lend itself to an objective approach? The short answer from some readers will be a resounding "no," but the carefully considered response might allow for the possibility in certain carefully selected circumstances.

For those of you who wish to learn more about this model, I suggest that you read the following books which are included in the endnotes to this chapter and others:

Malcolm Knowles, *The Modern Practice of Adult Education: From Pedagogy to Andragogy*, Revised and Updated. Jerrold W. Apps, *Improving Practice in Continuing Education*.

Notes

1. Ralph W. Tyler, *Basic Principles of Curriculum and Instruction* (Chicago: University of Chicago Press, 1949).

2. Malcolm S. Knowles, *The Modern Practice of Adult Education: From Pedagogy to Andragogy* (Chicago: Follett, 1980).

3. Tyler, *Basic Principles of Curriculum and Instruction*, pp. 3-62.

4. Ibid., pp. 5-16.

5. Ibid., pp. 16-25.

6. Ibid., pp. 25-33.

7. Ibid., p. 33.

8. Ibid., p. 84.

9. Knowles, *The Modern Practice of Adult Education*, pp. 198-215.

10. Ibid., pp. 202-204.

11. Ibid., p. 202.

12. Ibid., p. 133.

13. Ibid.

14. Ibid., pp. 72-78.

15. Edgar J. Boone, *Developing Programs in Adult Education* (Englewood Cliffs, N.J.: Prentice-Hall, 1985), pp. 104-113.

16. This list is an adaptation and expansion of comments found in Knowles, *The Modern Practice of Adult Education*, pp. 223-226; Boone, *Developing Programs in Adult Education*, p. 161, and Quentin H. Gessner, "Planning Conferences, Seminars, and Workshops for Large Groups of Adults," in *Priorities in Adult Education*, ed. David B. Rauch (New York: Macmillan, 1972), pp. 199-200.

17. Knowles, *The Modern Practice of Adult Education*, p. 223.

18. Ibid., p. 224.

19. Ibid., p. 44.

20. David W. Johnson and Frank P. Johnson, *Joining Together: Group Theory and Group Skills*, 3rd ed. (Englewood Cliffs, N.J.: Prentice-Hall, 1987).

21. Hedley G. Dimock, *Groups: Leadership and Group Development*, rev. ed. (San Diego: University Associates, 1987).

22. James W. White, *Intergenerational Religious Education: Models, Theory, and Prescription for Interage Life and Living in the Faith Community* (Birmingham, Ala.: Religious Education Press, 1986).

23. Ibid., p. 99.

24. David A. Kolb, *Experiential Learning: Experience as the Source of Learning and Development* (Englewood Cliffs, N.J.: Prentice-Hall, 1984), pp. 4-34.

25. Bruce Joyce and Marsha Weil, *Models of Teaching*, 3rd ed. (Prentice-Hall: Englewood Cliffs, N.J., 1986), chapter 20.

26. Ibid., p. 377.

Chapter 8

Evaluation Of
Adult Religious Education

Evaluation has been a critical part of the educational process for many years. It provides the basis for decision making about program development for new activities and change for existing activities. It is a vital tool for the practicing adult religious educator.

The quality of the learning experiences which are provided for learners will depend, in part, on the evaluative information which is gathered to support quality planning and development. This is a task which must be done, and done well, to provide appropriate programing.

Adult educators have focused considerably more attention over the years on the process of "program" evaluation rather than learner evaluation. The reasons for this situation are more complex than we may think initially.

First we must consider the fact that the vast majority of adult learning does not involve accreditation for a degree, certificate, diploma, license, etc.[1] The fact that a teacher is not required to certify that a certain type of learning has taken place can be quite liberating. It also follows from this that non-credit programs and courses exist in large numbers. Non-credit learning activities do not require the degree of learner assessment which occurs in credit programs. It is clear from the research that acquisition of credit is not a major factor in much adult religious education.[2]

The second reason may be found in the fact that most adult education is not compulsory. This means that learner satisfaction is a more important factor to be considered, thus leading to the emphasis on high quality programing. The churches and most other organizations in North American society must rely on people's personal commitment to participate in educational activities for adults.

The third reason is that some adults do not wish to receive the type of negative feedback which was a part of earlier school experiences. One key aspect of the early interpretation of andragogy was its differentiation from pedagogy as described by Malcolm Knowles.[3] Indeed it is true that some adults have had quite unsuccessful experiences in school classrooms, and there is a conscious desire on the part of adult educators to avoid bringing back unnecessary memories.

These statements are not intended to reflect on the majority of school teachers who do an effective job with the majority of the learners in their classrooms. Rather they remind us of those whose lack of success is defined by a former student's illiteracy and the lack of other skills for living.

Perhaps an important factor we should consider is the discomfort which most adult educators feel when they are required to evaluate the learning of a diverse group of learners. We have come to the realization that each adult learner has a personal perception of the importance of learning. The individual learner must be respected. In the final analysis, they will decide the importance of what they have learned in spite of whatever may be said about it. The mature, responsible adult will make the decision with reference only to what he or she considers to be appropriate comments from a facilitative, supportive educator.

Malcolm Knowles,[4] Jerold Apps,[5] and other adult educators have provided us with a vast array of information and methodology for the evaluation of programs. Some methods work best when they are applied to traditional group learning contexts while others work equally well with the nontraditional models.

We also have the new approaches to evaluation which are described as naturalistic and responsive by Egon Guba and Yvonne Lincoln and other authors.[6] These authors note the relationship between evaluation and value.[7] It is necessary to consider the nature of "value" in the evaluation method. Something may be of value in its own right or in a context-free situation. Things may have value also in an applied or external sense according to Guba and Lincoln.[8] Another way to express this is in relation to the learner. The learner may feel that what is learned has a personal value which exceeds the value placed upon it by other people. It is important in the evaluation of adult religious education activities that we do not lose sight of the personal value which learning has for the learner.

The very nature of adult education in both traditional and alternative models requires that we pay considerable attention to the value the learner places upon his or her individual learning experience and whatever is learned during the experience. Certain alternative models provide an excellent base for this individual assessment insofar as the learning itself has a more individualistic component.

The traditional model and some alternative models which are based upon the group approach to learning (for example, the study circle) focus more attention on the group and less upon the individual. Group goals are important in group learning situations, but they are not the sole issue to be considered. This means that we must be more careful to consider the individual learner and the personal aspects of learning in the evaluation process. This will insure that a vital component is not lost to us.

In the school system, the personal component of evaluation is comprised of the assessment of the students' progress in learning based upon movement toward objectives. This is considered to be inappropriate in all but certain specific programs for adults. Only when the need can be quite clearly demonstrated will the learner accept being evaluated by other persons. Then we must consider other approaches than those utilized by the school or pedagogical model.

A FRAMEWORK FOR PROGRAM EVALUATION

It should be stated at the very beginning that evaluation is something which occurs throughout the process of an educational activity. It may happen in an informal manner, or it may occur on a formal basis. It is my view that the informal evaluation occurring during virtually all programs provides very helpful information. Chats during a coffee break or shared meal will often provide very useful information. Thoughts and reactions will occur as we observe the learning process to provide more information. The key is found often in the confirmation of any previously collected information and of the usefulness of the data.

There are a number of ways we can categorize evaluation activities. The traditional division, as popularized by Benjamin Bloom and his colleagues in the *Handbook on Formative and Summative Evaluation of Student Learning*,[9] involves the division of the activities into "formative" and "summative" evaluation. It is also possible to utilize the intervention points of evaluation into the learning process or the evaluation strategies in order to provide further categorizations within a framework.

"Formative" evaluation is a term for evaluation which provides an indication of future directions for parts or all of a specific program which is soon to begin or has begun already.[10] The similarity to needs identification in the traditional, school-based model is quite obvious.

"Summative" evaluation refers to the form of evaluation performed at the completion of a learning activity, course, or a program. It is intended to provide judgments about the program's merits.[11] The only difficulty which should occur in distinguishing between the two aspects is during evaluation interventions which take place in the middle parts of courses or programs.

Intervention points are a most useful means of categorization of evaluation for the thoughtful practitioner. There are three periods of time when evaluation should be considered; the period when the course is being planned, the period when the course is running, and the period after the course has been completed. Valuable information may be acquired during each period depending upon the nature of the learning activity.

Figure 1 identifies the particular categories of evaluation in relation to the process of course development, presentation, and summation of activities. This figure provides an overview of the process.

FIGURE 1: A THEORETICAL MODEL FOR THE EVALUATION OF TRADITIONAL ADULT EDUCATION COURSES

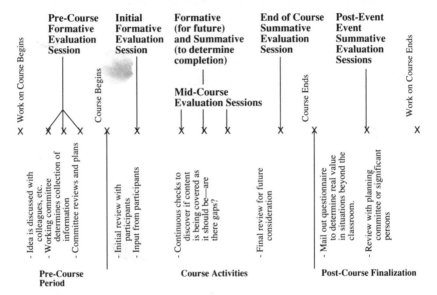

Examples of evaluation activities are provided on the left hand side of the figure for illustrative purposes.

No matter what form of evaluation we may consider, it is clear that the result must be found in learning. Learning is the central reference point on which planning, teaching, facilitation, administration, or evaluation is based. If this general point is kept in our thoughts throughout the process, we shall be able to perform the task effectively.

There are certain additional considerations to be made as we examine the issue of who should evaluate the learning. The learners, facilitators, planners, and external persons may all have a stake in the outcome of an evaluative process. These persons should be identified and involved in ways which are appropriate to the situation.

The learners will always have a stake in the outcome of an evaluation. As the clients of the program, they will wish to insure the availability of quality educational activities for themselves and others. The teacher or facilitator will be equally committed to quality for different but equally valid reasons.

METHODOLOGY

There are numerous informal and formal methods we can use for evaluating our programs. A genuine interest in the learner and skillful application of the methods will enable us to be effective evaluators. Informal methods will not be the focus of the chapter, but the information which is gathered in this fashion should not be neglected. An informal chat with learners will not only build the relationship which makes learners more open to communication but it may also supply considerable data.

The formal methods to be used could include the collection of information through questionnaires, interviews, and a contact group or committee. The size and nature of the group will determine the extent to which information is collected in a more personal manner or in a more distant impersonal manner. The larger or more distantly spread the group, the more likely the approach will be without the personal contact which provides a deeper understanding.

It is indeed fortunate that many church groups are relatively small and accessible. Although there are times when we need to consider the larger context, we shall have the opportunity to communicate more directly with people in small groups much of the time.

Please remember that some people communicate better in certain ways than others. Some persons prefer to write their comments while others are much happier to share them orally. There is also an important difference among the people who prefer oral communication insofar as some prefer to communicate directly on a one-to-one or very small group basis while others are quite comfortable in voicing their opinions in a larger group situation.

Questionnaire design is an acquired skill. It will take time to learn how to ask the right questions in the right way. We must consider the components of facilitation which impact upon the learning and then ask the questions which will assist us to improve our practice for the course being evaluated and future courses which will resemble it.

There are a number of helpful books with guides to help you develop the skills you require. I recommend that you read the works by Knowles, Apps, and Boone which were previously cited in this chapter. A very good book on questionnaire design was written some years ago by Douglas Berdie and John Anderson.[12]

A number of factors which influence the learning process have been identified over the years by various authors. It is stating the obvious to say that the program and the instructor(s) need to be evaluated. Also, the material resources may be most important in many learning situations. We should

Evaluation Sheet

Course _____

Date _____

Instructor _____

This evaluation will assist the organizers of this course to improve future programs for learners. We ask you to assist us in this important task. Please write your comments or place a check in the appropriate place.

A. Program Administration:

1. How did you find out about this course? _____

2. Did you have difficulties in gathering additional information about the course or in the registration procedures? _____
_____

3. Do you have any suggestions for improvement about the way in which the course was organized? _____
_____

B. Needs and Objectives:

Were the needs and objectives on which the program was based related to your needs and interests. Please rate the relationship on the following scale:
1 (virtually all fit) ____ 2 (most fit) ___ 3 (some fit) ____ 4 (few fit) ____ 5 (almost none fit) ___
Comments _____
_____

C. Program Design:

1. Which parts of the program, if any, helped you to learn the most? _____
_____
_____

2. Which parts of the program, if any, did not help your learning? _____
_____
_____

3. What suggestions do you have for change in future programs of this type? _____
_____
_____

D. Program Resources:

1. Please rate the instructor(s) on a scale of 1 to 5 on their ability to help you learn in this program:
1 (excellent) ___ 2 (very good) ___
3 (average) ___ 4 (below average) ___
5 (low)___.
Comments: _____
_____

2. Please rate the resource materials on a scale of 1 to 5 on their usefulness in helping you to learn in the program:
1 (excellent) ___ 2 (very good) ___
3 (average) ___ 4 (below average) ___
5 (low)___.
Comments: _____
_____

E. Please rate the evaluation procedures used to formulate changes during the program:
1 (excellent) ___ 2 (very good) ___
3 (average) ___ 4 (below average) ___
5 (low)___.
Suggestions for improvement _____
_____

F. Do you have any thoughts or suggestions which you wish to share with the evaluation team for this program? Please record them in the space provided: _____
_____
_____
_____

also consider the factors which lead up to the event and create a mental set. The physical environment in which learning happens will influence the situation as well.

The next problem involves obtaining the information without asking so many questions that learners become tired of evaluating the program. We do not wish to induce boredom or indifference to the process, thus the evaluation should be clearly relevant and economical.

The following points are critical to the formulation of good questionnaires (and, to a certain extent, interviews). You may wish to consider them carefully before proceeding with the development of evaluation forms:

1. State the purpose clearly at the beginning of the process.
2. Give clear directions for the procedures.
3. Use clear questions which will not confuse the reader.
4. Ask only those questions which are required to do the job.
5. Use open, unstructured questions for small groups.
6. Use structured questions for larger groups (ease of reading).
7. Have a clear category description for any rating scales. (excellent, very good, average, poor, etc.)
8. Evaluate all components which affect the learning situation.
9. Structure questionnaires to fit on one page if possible.
10. Give all parties to the learning an opportunity to evaluate.

If you follow these guidelines, your evaluation forms will provide you with information which will enable you to improve the quality of your programs and courses. See the example provided on the previous page.

Similar concerns need to be covered in the interview or group discussion for evaluation of a course. The advantage is that you will have the opportunity to correct misunderstandings or to interpret complex questions. The disadvantage of these face-to-face conversations is that the amount of ground to be covered is limited, as is the audience with which you will discuss the program or course.

Face-to-face discussions should be recorded as systematically as other forms of information. This may hamper your ability to communicate with the group. I suggest that a person who acts as recorder may help, or the compilation of information on sheets of newsprint or boards may help. The latter approach has the advantage of more group input and commitment, if that which is recorded is confirmed by the group

Notes

1. See Allen Tough, *The Adult's Learning Projects: A Fresh Approach to the Theory and Practice of Adult Learning*, 2nd ed. (Toronto: The Ontario Institute for

Studies in Education, 1979), p. 158.

2. R.E.Y. Wickett, "Adult Learning and Spiritual Growth," *Religious Education* 75: 5 (July-August, 1980) and R.E.Y. Wickett and G. Dunwoody, "The Religious Learning Projects of Catholic Adults in Early and Middle Adulthood," *Insight: A Journal of Adult Religious Education* 3 (1990), pp. 64-71.

3. See Malcolm S. Knowles, *The Modern Practice of Adult Education: Andragogy versus Pedagogy* (New York: Association Press, 1970), pp. 37-39.

4. Malcolm S. Knowles, *The Modern Practice of Adult Education: From Pedagogy to Andragogy* (Chicago: Follett, 1980), chapter 10.

5. See Jerold W. Apps, *Improving Practice in Continuing Education: Modern Approaches for Understanding the Field and Determining Priorities* (San Francisco: Jossey-Bass, 1985) and Jerold W. Apps, *How to Improve Adult Education in Your Church* (Minneapolis: Augsburg, 1972), pp. 83-86.

6. Egon G. Guba and Yvonne S. Lincoln, *Effective Evaluation: Improving the Usefulness of Evaluative Results through Responsive and Naturalistic Approaches* (San Francisco: Jossey-Bass, 1987).

7. Ibid., p. 39.

8. Ibid.

9. Benjamin S. Bloom, J. Thomas Hastings, and George F. Madaus, *Handbook on Formative and Summative Evaluation of Student Learning* (New York: McGraw-Hill, 1971).

10. Blaine R. Worthen and James R. Sanders, *Educational Evaluation: Alternative Approaches and Practical Guidelines* (New York: Longman, 1987), p. 34.

11. Ibid.

12. Douglas R. Berdie and John F. Anderson, *Questionnaires: Design and Use* (Methuchen, N.J.: Scarecrow, 1974).

Chapter 9

Intergenerational Religious Education

> This model combines the best features of the andragogical and pedagogical models. It enables the whole community to share in the educational process, thereby promoting a greater sense of wholeness and involvement. Combined and separate activities are interwoven in appropriate ways to insure an effective learning process.

This chapter will explore the area of adult religious education within the context of the multigenerational faith community. Many groups within our faith communities include families or other groups with more than one generation. Our learning may separate us at times, but it can also be used to bring us together. This chapter will discuss the ways in which we can attempt to achieve an integrated learning process for adults and children alike.

This particular model has been placed in proximity to the traditional model of andragogy because it appears to me to be basically compatible with that model. It has emerged from the field of religious education, while the other models in the book have their origins in adult education theory and practice.

This model incorporates the valid assumptions of the andragogical model which concern adults while also maintaining the elements essential to good pedagogy. Both children and adults can benefit from a model which brings them together as appropriate and allows them the chance to work separately when required.

Its similarities as a model are found in the common elements the andragogical model retained from pedagogy through its development. I refer here to the inclusion of such items as goals and objectives, a formal plan, and evaluation. These are familiar and often useful elements for many educators.

In a sense this model makes the family a type of group. There is still the formal group which is composed of the collective families and individuals, but the family becomes a sub-group within the context of the larger group. If we remember to work with the family as a special form of group, it may help us to be more effective educators.

James White has described a number of examples of intergenerational religious education through the ages.[1] One quite interesting example of a historical pattern of intergenerational religious education may be found in the Seder meal of the Jewish faith. This event provides an opportunity to teach through the meal's ritualistic questions and answers.[2] When I was given the opportunity some years ago as a Christian to participate in this event in the form of a simulation exercise, I found it to be a most rewarding experience.

White describes the potential use of four patterns of learning for intergenerational religious education in his book. The four patterns are "in-common experiences, parallel learning, contributive occasions, and interactive-sharing."[3] Each pattern can contribute to learning in a different way, and they need not be exclusive of each other. One could choose to use all four patterns in a sequence.

The first pattern, in-common experiences, White suggests can be invaluable in intergenerational programs.[4] All generations can identify with the shared experience although they will perceive it from their own points of view. This type of activity could be placed in the early part of a program.

Parallel learning refers to the situation in which people are separated for a period of time. Groups are separated by age in order to enable each group to learn in a manner best suited to their developmental levels. When they come back together, they will have learned about the same content and be able to share in the results.

Contributive occasions are those occasions when people come together to share something which has been created previously. This pattern will follow the parallel learning situation for many occasions.[5]

White suggests that the culmination of the process should involve a sharing of the results of the prior experiences by the various groups. This may be the heart of the matter for the author.[6] It features much that we could regard as integrative for the group as a whole as well as for the individual potentially.

The ideal program for White would involve all four components, as we see in the following Figure 1:[7]

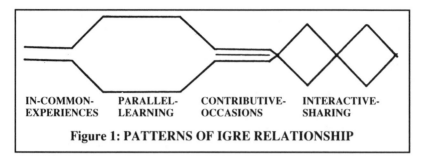

| IN-COMMON- | PARALLEL- | CONTRIBUTIVE- | INTERACTIVE- |
| EXPERIENCES | LEARNING | OCCASIONS | SHARING |

Figure 1: PATTERNS OF IGRE RELATIONSHIP

The order could follow quite readily from that which is found in the above figure.

White also describes what he calls six paradigms or "models" for the delivery of intergenerational religious education. These models include the family group (involving several families), the weekly class, the workshop, the seminar, the worship education program, and the camp.[8] Each model causes intergenerational interaction in a different way.

I am particularly intrigued by the concept of several families joining together. This situation would require access to strong external leadership in order to allow all members to participate fully.

The weekly class has long-term potential and, if held in conjunction with Sunday worship, brings together a larger number of participants. This was the type of situation in a congregation in which I chaired the Christian Education Committee several years ago.

White suggests himself that we do not have sufficient data for the most rigorous evaluation of intergenerational educational programs.[9] Anecdotal and other forms of program evaluation, including the "hard" data of attendance figures, tend to be used to justify our use of a model. It would be helpful if we had more information about learning outcomes, but busy practitioners do not always have the time or the inclination to collect such data.

It is not my intention to describe several models in this chapter. I shall describe one model which is slightly broader in nature than the ones described by James White. This will involve a process of integration which I trust will not violate the basic concepts of that author. This proposed model relies heavily upon the work of White, nevertheless I accept the shortcomings which arise from the adaptive process.

This will be a flexible model which can be used for workshops or classes. It may contain elements of worship, but I should prefer not to require such activities. Some denominations may prefer to separate these activities for their own reasons.

METHODOLOGY

The following is a general outline of the stages of intergenerational program activities to be followed by the organizers (See Figure A):

1. Planning should involve a team with representatives of all age groups to be involved in the learning insofar as this is possible.

2. The plans should be shared as widely as possible to insure acceptance and support.

3. Resource persons should be selected for their ability to work with the various groups of participants as well as their knowledge and skill.

4. When the plans have been made and approved, information should be circulated to families and persons of all age groups.

5. Initial activities, including climate setting, should be designed to make all participants feel involved and accepted.

6. The activities for learning should involve all parties of whatever age group is present. Separation of age groups should occur where needed and as little as possible.

7. Evaluation should be appropriate and involve input from all participants in the learning experience.

8. There should be some form of culminating event or activity to enable the learning to end with a positive experience, perhaps in worship.

Figure A:

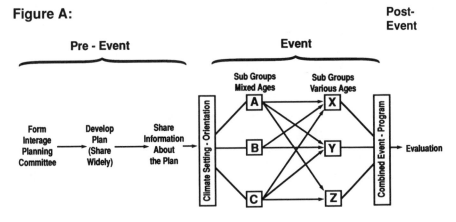

Intergenerational Program

The planning process should take into account all age levels. It would be appropriate to form a planning group where all age groups could contribute to the process. Where this is not possible, ideas should be gathered from all groups by a representational planning committee. Plans should be reviewed for acceptability and appropriateness by the groups after they are formulated.

There are certain critical issues which should be considered in this planning process. Perhaps the most important of these involves the applicability to the various age groups. The key question to ask about each part of the plan is, "How will the (children, teenagers, young adults, or older adults) react?" If any of these groups will not respond fully and positively to a planned activity, reconsideration should occur to alter it or to exclude it or to arrange parallel events.

Another critical issue of planning is how to involve all age groups. The youngest may not be able to participate fully, nor will it always be possible to have a representative from each group. It is not necessary to defer planning an activity if it is not possible to have all parties involved. Perhaps representatives from certain groups will find themselves attracted to future planning committees if successful events occur.

The issue of broad consultation is important, particularly if the committee is only partially representative of the community. Every effort should be made to share the ideas and plans for response and potential feedback prior to implementation.

Resource persons plus the discussion and activity group leaders should be chosen for their flexibility as well as their ability to relate effectively to the different age groups. This is not an easy type of person to find but the ability to work with children, youth, young, middle, and older adults is a definite asset.

A resource person who is both flexible and personable will be the most effective asset one can find for a course. I believe that it is particularly important to find people who do not speak "down" to any group, particularly children. There is a skill in communication which allows the leader to speak appropriately to all groups.

Insure that families will participate by advertising and by physical and other arrangements. Accessibility will be a factor for the younger and the older persons. A commitment to support this accessibility may be required from those who can provide transport.

It is important that all parties be made to feel that they are fully involved participants in the learning through the climate setting process. The way in which the learning begins will allow generations which do not always feel completely welcome or involved to gain those positive feelings.

Exercises or activities should be chosen to incorporate by being attractive and appropriate for all generations represented. I feel, for example, that "memory games" do not fit all age groups, but friendly and informal introductions or simple drawing exercises for symbolic introductions may be suitable and enjoyable for all.

The advantage of mixing groups is that we can insure the intergenerational effect. If we do this as much as possible, we are more likely to achieve this result. Groups may still be separated when the need exists for this to occur. This is as true of the introductory exercises as it is of later group activities.

I like to see creative activities which include all age groups as part of this process. To do something new will challenge and stimulate all parties. If the correct activities are chosen, the members of the various age groups will have something different to contribute. Adults may excel in the totality of their experience and knowledge against that of the child, but the child will often bring some unique insight into a creative process. The lack of experience may permit fresh insight which can be combined with the adults' insight based on their prior experience to solve creative problems.

The difficulty of mixed groups is that the content must be delivered to all participants in an appropriate manner. This naturally means that it may require a format which does little to stretch or challenge the thoughts of certain groups while providing what is needed by another group.

The division of the community into age groups will permit each group to be taken further in relation to their interests in the content than would otherwise be possible. So, do it! Do it without reservation when the situation calls for it. Simply avoid the division on unnecessary or inappropriate grounds.

The activities which bring the learning to a close might include a worship activity or some shared celebration. There is some merit in merriment! If we wish people to return in the future to the activities we plan, this can be a very positive way to end the experience we wish them to share in again.

Any evaluative procedures should involve all parties. The planning committee should have the broad representation to allow it to perform this task. A larger planning committee may choose to have a sub-committee perform this function while a smaller planning committee may retain the responsibility.

A key issue here is the ability of each group to contribute in an appropriate manner. The youngest may be asked to say what they liked and didn't like. Others may complete forms, but I still prefer verbal input as part of the feedback process. The use of small group sessions divided into appropriate groups for communication may provide the best insight.

SUMMARY COMMENTS

This model can be used effectively where there is a diversity of age groups within the faith community. Provided that there are no factors within the community which inhibit such interage activities, the model will assist in the development of cohesion and nonexclusive relationships.

Avoidance of the use of this model is suggested where there are strong community factors which mitigate against interage inclusion in activities. Such factors might include strong community norms or feelings concerning appropriateness.

The model will work best in faith communities with large numbers of families which recognize the need to be inclusive. Where there is the desire to share experience and to build relationships with all parts of the community, this model can provide a sound basis. This should not be confused with the models which build toward community action, as the emphasis is on relationship rather than action here.

The disadvantages of the model include the difficulty of working across several generations. Do not believe that this will be a simple process, as its complexity cannot be underrated. Where adults expect their needs to be paramount, this model will not respond to that expectation.

This type of activity has been successful in many faith communities over the years. James White has given us a most adequate basis for a successful approach to interage learning. For future reference and further learning about this model, the suggested resource is his book, listed in the notes.

Notes

1. James W. White, *Intergenerational Religious Education: Models, Theory, and Prescription for Interage Life and Learning in the Faith Community* (Birmingham, Ala.: Religious Education Press, 1988), chapter 4.
2. Ibid., pp. 71-72.
3. Ibid., pp. 26-30.
4. Ibid., p. 27.
5. Ibid., pp 9-28.
6. Ibid., pp. 28-29.
7. Ibid., p. 29.
8. Ibid., p. 33.
9. Ibid., p. 225.

Chapter 10

Alternative Models: Why We Use Them

This chapter follows from our discussions of two traditional models and leads into the description of the alternative models for adult religious education. The andragogical model clearly owes its origins to early research and the practice in the field of adult education prevalent into the 1970s. We have commented on its use with reference to adult religious education, but there is a need to recognize its limitations.

Alternative models provide us with an opportunity to move beyond the limits of the andragogical model. The value of these models is that we can use them to overcome the limits of that model. Our facilitational practice becomes more diversified and thus more effective as we work with a wider range of people through the use of alternative models.

Perhaps the most important reason for using alternative models is the diversity of activities people undertake in order to learn. We know that learning occurs at times in the traditional classroom situation with groups and organized programs. But we have long suspected, and research has confirmed the fact, that learning also occurs in many contexts.

When we examine the research and writings of Allen Tough[1] and authors such as Stephen Brookfield,[2] Patrick Penland,[3] and many others, we can see the richness and variety of adult learning which occurs outside as well as within the classroom. Brookfield presents a very comprehensive overview of the research on self-directed learning.[4] Cyril Houle[5] provides a useful review of certain case studies of active, individual learning. If all these authors have interpreted the results of their research in order to give us one clear message, it might be to the effect that we should not ignore learning outside the course and class context.

The adult's inability to learn at times in the traditional classroom context is illustrated partly by the fact that many adults have not achieved the basic skills required for literacy and numeracy in our schools. It is also true that a majority of adults do not engage in formal classes in adult education. Studies from Johnstone and Rivera in the 1960s[6] to the recent report, *One in Every Five*,[7] indicate that a minority of the population will participate in formal adult education courses.

We should consider also the extent to which adults wish to learn about a diverse range of substantive content areas. The range of areas will make it necessary for us to consider alternatives because the way to teach content will be influenced by its very nature. We do not teach attitudes in the same way as we teach skills, and the reverse of that statement is also true.

My own research has convinced me that people have an infinitely wider capacity to examine the religious issues than many educators are likely to have. I was amazed constantly by the variety of areas to which people referred when describing their learning for spiritual growth and development.[8] This variety cannot be addressed by limited, traditional programing.

An additional factor, which may be more important than any of the others, is the extent to which individual or "group" differences will influence learning. Educational psychologists have long suggested that there are "personality" types which must be considered in the teaching/learning process. Such authors as Gordon Lawrence[9] and Carolyn Mamchur[10] have interpreted these important differences based upon Jungian personality types for educators.

The end result of this discussion is that I feel that we must see learning in a broader framework. It is no longer possible for us to offer the traditional course on Holy Scriptures or "How to visit the shut-in." We need to consider the content and its nature and, even more important, the learner and his or her nature. Having done this review of the situation, we need to be able to choose from a variety of options in order to achieve the optimum possible results.

The remainder of this chapter will provide an overview of the alternative models to be presented in subsequent chapters. A fuller description of each model will be contained in the individual chapters, but the overview may assist you to place each particular model within a more general framework.

MODELS FOR INDIVIDUAL LEARNING

The need for individuals to learn and grow will be a critical part of learning in our society. In some instances, that learning will occur in a group context, but the most frequent form of learning appears to be learning which the individual performs in an independent, individualized, and self-directed manner.[11] Whether we refer to this as self-education or self-directed learning or whatever, we should recognize the existence of this process in order to assist the learner in any possible way.

Many individuals will need the individual activity and the freedom and flexibility which comes from that situation in order to learn what they require. When people reach a particular moment in their lives when something is important, we should encourage that pursuit rather than trying to detract or force it into our mold.

Please remember that there will be times when it is not possible to create a group situation, even when the individual learner would prefer that situation. We can provide an alternative that will enable learning instead of surrendering to the circumstances and giving up.

The models which are described in chapters 11, 12, and 13 are the Independent Learning Model, the Learner-Centered Model, and the Learning Covenant Model. They provide us with examples of effective ways to recognize and work with individual learners. They provide us with ways to organize resources and our own interactions. If we wish to be effective in our work with a wide range of adult learners, we must include these models in our repertoire of activities.

MODELS FOR GROUPS AND INDIVIDUAL LEARNING

The individual in our society frequently wants to engage in group activities to enable and support his or her learning. These models will provide alternative approaches which recognize both the nature of adulthood and adult patterns of group learning.

The focus is on the learning of the individual through involvement with a group. There is every intention that the adult who participates in this learning will take from the process that which he or she needs to learn.

The Learning Covenant model which is used in a group is a perfect example of what we are discussing in this section. Learners may learn individually and in one-to-one contract situations or they may have individual contracts which were developed in the group context. The end result is individual learning, but the process involves the support of a group as well as a facilitator.

The reasons why people join groups in order to support their learning are numerous. Social reinforcement, opportunity for discussion, and access to resources would rank along with familiarity as valid reasons. We should recognize these reasons and incorporate group models which incorporate them into the process. The end result, however, must be that individuals will meet their own needs.

Chapters 13, 14, and 15 describe the "Tip of the Iceberg" Model, the Interdependent Group Model, as well as the previously mentioned Learning Covenant Model. The group will often raise the comfort level of the individual as well as the learning skills, but the group's goals will be subject to the commitment of each individual.

MODELS FOR SOCIAL ACTION

The following models in chapters 16, 17, and 18 provide an opportunity for groups to learn and grow together. These models include the Scandinavian Study Circle, Freire's "Pedagogy" Model, and the Action-Research Model. An ultimate goal of these models may be described as social or community action. They create the process which may culminate in social action.

The presupposition behind these models is not that individuals are unimportant. The contrary is true. The presupposition behind these models is that the needs of the individual will be met ultimately in the context of a strong community of learners and as the result of joint activity.

One important aspect of these models is the democratic component. Each model designed to facilitate the joint action of group members must contain an element which fosters democratic analysis and decision making. The following models all demonstrate this element quite adequately for our purposes.

Another important element in these models is the extent to which each attempts to support feelings of self-worth among the learners. To have truly democratic action, one must have people who feel that their contribution counts. These models do recognize this component.

There are those who would suggest that the Scandinavian Study Circle ought to be placed in the previous section. Their views are testimony to the flexibility of this model. I have chosen to place it in this section because of its ability to bring learners together in a highly democratic process with the strong potential for social action.

Those adult religious educators who choose to utilize these models must have a commitment to social action. If your sense of commitment is severely limited or nonexistent, choose another approach. The personal commitment to facilitate is always important but it is critical in this instance. Either the process will not work because the commitment is insufficient or there will be considerable unhappiness with both the process and the results.

A belief in the need for social justice in society is seen by many as vital to these models. A broadly based concept of the role of people in the political process in order to achieve justice is essential. If you do not trust the collective wisdom, beware the model which is based upon respect for the collective wisdom of people.

DISTANCE EDUCATION

This model stands alone because of its particular, special circumstances. Its very nature requires us to work quite differently with the learner. Yet there are things we can learn from other models and situations, as we review this model. Chapter 19 will focus on certain distance education activities with reference to current work in the field.

The Open University in Britain and other work in distance education will be cited in order to suggest a comprehensive and efficient model for distance education in religious studies for adults. My recent appointment as a visiting professor at the Open University has increased my knowledge of the internal operation of that well-known institution.

SUMMARY COMMENTS

Now that you have an idea about the way the models may be used, you may choose to read the chapters most relevant to your learners and your situation. If it is not possible to form groups in your situation in order to learn about certain topics, the individualized models may suit your purposes. Remember that the very fact that it is possible to form a group should not preclude the possibility of individualized activity.

Should you see social action as the appropriate result of the learning activities, you will want to examine the three chapters which review the Study Circle, Freieran, and the Action-Research Models. Please make a decision to use these models only after careful thought and consideration.

The models are yours to consider and utilize as you choose. More information is available about each model, and references are to be found in each chapter which will enable you to move beyond this book.

Notes

1. Allen Tough, *The Adult's Learning Projects: A Fresh Approach to Theory and Practice in Adult Education*, 2nd ed. (Toronto: The Ontario Institute for Studies in Education, 1971).

2. Stephen D. Brookfield, *Understanding and Facilitating Adult Learning* (San Francisco: Jossey-Bass, 1986), pp. 147-165.

3. Patrick R. Penland, *Self-Planned Learning in America* (Pittsburgh: Book Center, Graduate School of Library and Information Science, University of Pittsburgh, 1977).

4. Brookfield, *Understanding and Facilitating Adult Learning*, pp. 148-150.

5. Cyril O. Houle, *Patterns of Learning: New Perspectives on Life-Span Education* (San Francisco: Jossey-Bass, 1984).

6. J.W.C. Johnstone and R.J. Rivera, *Volunteers for Learning: A Study of the Educational Pursuits of American Adults* (Chicago: Aldine, 1965).

7. M.S. Devereux, *One in Every Five: A Survey of Adult Education in Canada* (Ottawa, Canada: Statistics Canada and Education Support Sector, Department of the Secretary of State, 1985).

8. R.E.Y. Wickett, "Adult Learning and Spiritual Growth," *Religious Education* 75: 5 (July-August, 1980), pp. 452-461 and R.E.Y. Wickett and Gregory Dunwoody, "The Religious Learning Projects of Catholic Adults in Early and Middle Adulthood," *Insight: A Journal of Adult Religious Education* 3 (1990), pp. 66-71.

9. Gordon Lawrence, *People Types and Tiger Stripes: A Practical Guide to Learning Styles*, 2nd ed. (Gainesville, Fla.: Center for Applications of Psychological Type, 1982).

10. Carolyn M. Mamchur, *Insights: Understanding Yourself and Others* (Toronto: The Ontario Institute for Studies in Education Press, 1984).

11. See Tough, *The Adult's Learning Projects*, and Wickett, "Adult Learning and Spiritual Growth."

Chapter 11

The Independent Learner

We need to find ways to support the person who pursues learning in his or her own individual way. Courses and groups cannot
be provided for all learners in all areas of potential learning. A system of accessible resources can be designed to provide maximum assistance to the individual learner.

Why should there be a chapter on this particular character who goes about
his or her daily affairs without taking a course, participating in a group, or
seeking our wise counsel and direction? Do we really need to concern ourselves with this strange person and what do we do if we are concerned? I
believe that we should consider the requirements of these persons who are frequently members of our faith community who have chosen the "independent"
approach to their learning.

The independent learner is a somewhat separated companion in the journey on the road of growth and development. He or she is attempting to come
to terms with many of the same issues as other persons who are engaging in
this same journey while involved with the adult religious educator or some
other "educator." The journey is no easier for those who need to travel it
alone.

Cyril Houle has provided the background for this model in his first category of educational situations, the "independent study" category.[1] He describes
this type of learning as "learning which must be guided at every point by the
individualism of the learner."[2] The difference between this model and other
models which incorporate elements of self-direction lies in the extent to
which others become involved in the process. This model has the lowest
level of external involvement.

Houle suggests that the information for this form is highly anecdotal,[3] but I believe that the subsequent research in self-directed learning cited elsewhere in this volume, including this chapter, has helped us to understand the situation. We do have clear evidence of the existence of independent learning or study and, in my opinion, the need to understand and respond to the requirements of learners who pursue it out of choice or necessity.

My thoughts in respect of independent learning go back to the journey of the apostle Paul, as described in the Christian tradition. I think of a man who was involved in the persecution of a new religious group but who must have understood the new religion in order to perform his jobs as prosecutor and persecutor. His journey must have been quite lonely as the doubts about the validity of his actions began to creep into his mind.

Paul must have needed to acquire knowledge of the "heresy" which he was required to destroy. He must have been puzzled by the strange attitudes of these followers of Christ based upon this new form of religion. His own changing attitudes and the need to comprehend what was happening to him would have involved significant learning.

There could have been no confidante for Paul as he searched for truth. To admit uncertainty would have invited disaster. His position as an authority figure with major responsibilities would have been threatened by the least indication of doubt. He had no opportunities to share his thoughts, especially the important doubts.

Yet we know that Paul had his doubts. He had to come to terms with them eventually. He had to discover the truth within his own mind in order to satisfy his own innermost feelings. In the end, he was able to do what he had to do in spite of all obstacles. He had "the courage to be," in the view of the author, Paul Tillich.[4]

I am not suggesting that all independent learners are in the same position as Paul, although there may be some situations in some countries where this is the case. I wish to suggest that there are many different and worthwhile journeys in process and that these journeys should be supported and recognized.

We cannot give permission for these journeys nor can we guide along the way in a subtle or direct manner. What we can do is recognize the journey and be open to whatever possibilities exist for us to assist as the journey progresses.

I should like to suggest also that there are very few learners who are totally "independent" persons. We might suggest that there are a large number of adults with an orientation toward independence in the learning process. Yet it is difficult to imagine learning which is totally independent of all external resources. Tough and other researchers have found that adults often require assistance in various ways with their self-directed learning.[5]

Clearly this group of independent learners will fall into the category of self-directed in their orientation toward learning. They will exhibit the characteristics of self-direction and of what Witkin has described as "field independent" persons.[6] They will be inner-directed and have a strong sense of self-identity.

When we talk about "independent learners" we often have an image of the individual working in isolation from facilitators, teachers, or other learners. The human side of the resource base is emphasized to the neglect of the material or nonhuman side of the resource base.

Most independent learners are interacting with resources which are nonhuman in nature during the learning process. They are dependent on these resources to the extent that they are helpful in the learning process.

It may be true to state that the independent learner may wish to relate to other persons at certain times during the process. This would involve a limited interaction which would not reduce their feeling of independence but it would enable the learning. The research of Wickett[7] and Dunwoody[8] indicated that adult learners engaged in religious learning believe that their learning projects could have been improved by opportunities to discuss. I believe that adult religious educators should make themselves both accessible and available for such opportunities as the learner requires.

If you accept this premise, that independent learners are not totally independent but partially dependent, you will be able to accept the possibility that they can be helped. The nature of the assistance must be quite in keeping with the nature of their choice of learning process. That is to say, the assistance must be unobtrusive and nondirective.

Suitability and accessibility are two key words which describe the resources needed by this group. The methodology for the facilitation of this type of learning involves the creation of an accessible resource base which meets the needs of the independent learner.

The arrival of new forms of technology to assist the learner to access information, skills, or other items will be of immense value to many persons, if they have the ability to utilize the technology. Literature searches on computer systems and other processes will enable the learner to obtain what he or she requires when sources are not otherwise readily accessible. A well-stocked resource center will provide on site and electronically accessible items.

Please remember that you will have no say in the way this learner will begin and proceed with the learning. If you wish to assist the learner, you will not assume that he or she wishes to move to an alternative, more dependent methodology. If they do wish to do so and they believe that you are open to the possibility, they will tell you. Only then will you be able to utilize the contents of another chapter.

METHODOLOGY

The methodology of this model is different from that of any other model in various ways. At times, it may appear to be a non-methodology, but I prefer to think of it as a methodology of preparation. What I am suggesting is the methodology of organizing the situation in order to respond to the learner as he or she requires.

There will be three parts to the methodology of assisting the independent learner. The first is to provide access to the resources which will be needed. The second phase will insure that the learner can utilize the resource base which has been created. The third phase is personal availability on the part of the adult religious educator.

The type of resources which are to be made available to the learner will depend in large part upon the type of situation in which the sponsoring church or agency finds itself. Finances and physical facilities will determine part of what can be done. I propose that a committee be formed and that consensus decision making be used to determine what can and should be done.

Most resources will cost something, although gifts and donations may be obtained to enable greater opportunities for acquisition. If the plans for the resource base can be seen by the community to have value to many, there will be an opportunity to obtain the appropriate items.

A variety of resource bases needs to be incorporated into our system in order to meet the potential needs of learners. We should consider both the traditional print media as well as the electronic print media. The need for the visual, non-print option also exists because of the persons who learn more effectively through these alternatives. Films, video tapes, etc. should be purchased and made available.

We all know that the traditional printed materials are the most familiar and useful resources for many adult learners. Books, pamphlets, journals, etc., can be utilized by many learners. The variety of materials to be made available should be selected carefully with both the needs of the institutional context and the diverse interests of prospective learners in mind.

The advantages of this resource base are that it is both diverse and plentiful. You will have so much to choose from that the choices will become difficult at times. There are also problems of storage and access which may need to be overcome.

The electronic print media is an evolving source which can be accessed in an incredibly quick manner. The requirement is simply to have a computer with the capability to relate via telephone to other computers. This is simply a means to access data bases existing throughout our world. A personal computer with a modem for telephone connection and a printer for converting what is displayed on screen to the printed page is all that is needed. Such items have become remarkably affordable in recent years. You can have many extras at a higher price, but you will be paying for speed, complexity, and better printed copy.

The material from the electronic data bases is communicated in print. It arrives to be displayed on screen or, via a printer, on a page. It is my contention that we shall find it necessary in the future to utilize such complex systems of storage and retrieval for our systematized printed material. Discs use less space than printed pages and bound volumes.

Both the traditional printed materials and the electronic printed materials have a serious limitation. They are inaccessible to the functionally illiterate or those persons of low levels of literacy. It is for this reason that I advise an alternative source such as the film or video tape which relies on the visual image to express the idea or the audio tape with the spoken word.

There will be limits upon the availability of materials, but creative institutions are prepared to meet the challenge. Contact national and regional organizations to gain lists of available films and tapes. The increase in the number of personal video cassette players will enable learners to use materials from our resource centers and those of others.

Study guides are not likely to be popular with this group, although other learners may choose to make use of them. If the study guide contains materials which can be used flexibly by the learner, there is then no need to follow it precisely, and an independent learner may adapt the material to his or her use.

Select visual and oral materials for their quality and relevance. The choice of materials will impact upon the extent to which learners will utilize your resource base. Budgetary limitations will vary from one institution to another, but the dividends to be derived from careful choice are considerable.

Please remember that the resource base which you are creating for the independent learner will be available also to the other learners and facilitators of programs. The great advantage of the modern resource center is that it can access resources well beyond its immediate location at reasonable cost.

SUMMARY COMMENTS

This model works where it is preferable to the learner or there is no other more appropriate model. It is a model which is chosen by the learner, not the educator. You will not be able to choose which learner to work with in this model, only whether or not you intend to be involved in any way with the learner.

A willingness to work with those who undertake the journey of learning in less traditional and independent ways will give good results in the end. The view which may help us to accept this approach to learning is one which recognizes the important internal or external forces which compel the learner to take the journey. If we believe that "something or someone of importance" is driving them to learn, we can accept more readily the need and the resulting activity.

The disadvantages to the facilitator are easily identified. We feel out of touch and of little help most of the time. If we can adjust to these feelings, helpful people that we are, we may be ready to provide assistance at the moment when it is required.

Learners will also experience disadvantages in this model. They may feel the same isolation without the possibility of contact with other learners which is experienced by the facilitator. Should this feeling of isolation become too great, it is possible that the learner will seek the contact which will help to overcome it.

This model is not without its advantages. It is possible to serve a wider group through the provision of a resource base without strings. Our courses may not appeal to all, but time and energy are required to organize and facilitate them. Sufficient energy may not be available to run all required activities. It is also true that some will only learn in this manner. We must serve the interest of the whole community as best we can.

The effectiveness of this model will be determined by the learner in the final analysis. Perhaps the best way for an educator to know about this issue of effectiveness is to ask the user of your resources and to observe the nature of the utilization patterns. I believe that this model will be effective if properly implemented.

Notes

1. Cyril O. Houle, *The Design of Education* (San Francisco: Jossey-Bass, 1972), pp. 91-96.

2. Ibid., p. 96.

3. Ibid., p. 91.

4. Paul Tillich, *The Courage to Be* (New Haven: Yale University Press, 1952).

5. Allen Tough, *The Adult's Learning Projects: A Fresh Approach to the Theory and Practice of Adult Learning*, 2nd ed. (Toronto: Ontario Institute for Studies in Education, 1979), pp. 105-122.

6. H.A. Witkin, "The Nature and Importance of Individual Differences in Perception," *Journal of Personality* 18 (1949), pp. 145-170 and H.A. Witkin, "Individual Differences in Ease of Perception of Embedded Figures," *Journal of Personality* 19 (1950), pp. 1-15.

7. R.E.Y. Wickett, "Adult Learning and Spiritual Growth," *Religious Education* 75: 5 (July-August, 1980), pp. 452-461.

8. G. Dunwoody, "A Descriptive Survey of Important Religious Learning Projects of Roman Catholic Adults in Early and Middle Adulthood." (Unpublished Manuscript, circa 1987) and R.E.Y. Wickett and Gregory Dunwoody, "The Religious Learning Projects of Catholic Adults in Early and Middle Adulthood," *Insight: A Journal of Adult Religious Education* 3 (1990), p. 71.

Chapter 12

The Learner-Centered Model

This model is adapted from the writings of Carl Rogers based
upon a suggestion in a book by C.O. Houle. It provides a basis for
a one-to-one relationship between the facilitator and the learner.
The degree of structure in this model is minimal. The stress is on
support as opposed to direction.

The intention of this chapter and this part of the book is to review certain
forms of relationships which may facilitate one-to-one learning. It is appropriate for you to review these options in situations where the content should
be considered in a limited context or where there are insufficient numbers of
students to warrant any form of group involvement in the learning process.

The title of the model was chosen because of its similarity to the approaches to counseling and teaching of Carl Rogers. If Rogers' approach to counseling can be seen as "client-centered," this model is learner-centered in its
nondirective approach. Please note that this model is an *adaptation* based upon
ideas taken from Carl Rogers.

Bruce Joyce and Marsha Weil provide a description of a Rogerian model
in their volume entitled, *Models of Teaching*.[1] The model I am proposing
diverges more from the therapeutic model than is the case for Joyce and
Weil. I shall leave you to judge which is truer to Rogers' original approach
and more appropriate for your use.

It is seldom the case that learners appear in large numbers to consider
every topic or issue which can involve learning, nor should we expect the
same level of commitment of time and energy from each person who express-
es an interest in something. The commitment from one person may exceed

that of others. If we neglect the option of individual learning activities, we shall miss many opportunities for the facilitation of relevant learning.

The situation in many small congregations is particularly suited to this type of learning. Rural areas where there are small numbers of people to begin with will find this approach to be most conducive to meeting needs which would otherwise remain unmet. A wide variety of needs and interests with minimal overlap may make it necessary to consider individual members on a one-to-one basis.

It should also be stated that there are a number of content areas where there is a need for the learning process to be individualized. The content may be highly personal in nature. Should the learning need involve an issue such as a personal tragedy or a crisis of faith, individual attention may be required. If the learner would feel uncomfortable in a discussion with more than one other person or where someone other than a qualified professional was involved, the one-to-one situation should be utilized to prevent potential discomfort and to maximize the possibilities for learning.

My own research in the area of learning projects related to spiritual growth revealed learning situations related to marital breakdown, alcoholism, and the death of a significant other person.[2] These situations often require the privacy of a one-to-one relationship and the sensitivity of a trained professional to support the learning process.

This method should not be used in situations where the learner requires a considerable amount of direction. Those situations will clearly benefit from a facilitational procedure with a more directive and focused approach. There will be learners who wish to have a greater degree of facilitator direction. When their attitudes to the facilitator reflect this situation and a one-to-one situation is still appropriate, move to the level of other-directed relationship which is needed.

C. O. Houle has defined four different categories of one-to-one relationships for teaching/learning situations in his book, *The Design of Education.*[3] These categories are characterized by varying degrees of learner and/or facilitator responsibility for control of the learning process.

I believe that the approach which takes the maximum level of responsibility and control and places them in the hands of the learner is quite similar to the styles of facilitation and counseling developed by Carl Rogers.[4] Rogers' views involve the individual at the center of the process of learning with the facilitator as somewhat peripheral and supportive rather than controlling. Roger's view of the process of psychotherapy and counseling also gives considerable insight into the ways the facilitator should operate. If we believe that certain aspects of the counseling process involve learning on the part of the client, we can see the resemblance between the two areas of activity.

The views of Rogers on the interpersonal relationship between facilitators and learners are indicated in his book, *Freedom to Learn in the '80's*. He makes it clear that the facilitator should have certain attitudes toward the learner.[5] These qualities include the ability to develop a "real" relationship with the learner, one which is without a false front. The facilitator should also value and trust the learner.

On Becoming a Person, which is a book on the nature of the person and how others should relate to the person, describes the characteristics appropriate for a counselor. I believe that they can be summarized, based on his writings, to include the following abilities:

1. The ability to accept and respect the client.
2. The ability to speak and act clearly and sensitively.
3. The ability to free oneself from the past and the institutional framework.[6]

I regard these characteristics or abilities as equally applicable to this model and its facilitator.

Perhaps the most difficult quality of Rogers' facilitator is the quality of empathy. This involves a sensitive awareness of the feelings of the learner. This quality will enable a very high level of understanding of the learner's actions in the learning process.

The added factor is normally the extent to which the facilitator ascribes to the possibilities for learners to be successful in learning with minimal guidance. A person who feels that he or she should guide the learner in the process at all times is not likely to provide opportunities for self-direction. That person will choose the most directive form of one-to-one relationship. A person who believes in the potential of the individual to perform the learning activities in a satisfactory manner will see the possibilities inherent in the less controlling methods.

There is one very important difference between the counseling process and the process of facilitating learning which has implications for the interactive process of facilitator and learner. Rogers indicates quite clearly the value of questioning to assist the learning process in his book, *Freedom to Learn for the '80's*.[7]

Rogers does cite evidence of the effectiveness of "open" teaching from studies by Horowitz[8] and Walberg et al.,[9] in order to indicate the value of this approach to education.[10] He clearly regarded his approach to facilitation as an "open" approach.

If Rogers was uncertain about his ability to "teach" anyone anything of true significance in his life, it should also be stated that he has been present in many forms (in person, books, videos, and so on) while many people have engaged in considerable learning of personal importance. Perhaps this is a factor to be considered by all of us as we think about our relationships with learners. Our involvement may involve a simple act of presence while whatever we have to offer is placed at the learner's disposal.

METHODOLOGY

A considerable amount of learning about this method may come through an examination of the Rogerian method of counseling. The similarities are worth considering insofar as it is possible to see the counseling process as one which involves learning. Who would doubt that most approaches to counseling involve the gain of a new understanding?

The following steps provide an overview of the process to be undertaken in the implementation of this model:

1. Build a relationship which includes an indication of acceptance and support.
2. Use good questioning techniques and *listen* to the answers.
3. Organize meetings at appropriate and mutually agreeable times.
4. Have resource materials available at meetings based on the answers to your questions.
5. Be prepared to get more involved, if the learner so desires.
6. Help the learner to bring the relationship to an appropriate closure.
7. Indicate future resources and information to assist continued learning as requested by the learner.

The initial meetings of the one-to-one, nondirective approach are critical in the determination of future success in this method. It has been noted that this is important to the Rogerian approach to counseling and facilitation.

Considerable time and effort should be put into the process of building the new relationship. Have no doubt that this will be a new form of relationship even if you have a prior relationship with the learner in other contexts. This new form of relationship will provide an opportunity to explore new dimensions of activity which, if successful, will enhance your relationship.

The learner is normally aware of the desire for support in the learning process and of the fact that the chosen facilitator has a certain background normally required to provide the support. What the learner needs to know is whether or not the appropriate form of support will be forthcoming. He or she may wish to confirm details about the facilitator's area of expertise to insure a "fit."

The skills of a good counselor are most useful in the initial meetings because the development of the relationship often requires good listening skills as well as the ability to ask the appropriate questions to gain new information. An awareness of the learner's needs and interests and of the process which the learner wishes to follow are combined with the process of relationship building. In fact, the way one proceeds with the meeting will be to pursue these questions in a manner which enables the development of the relationship.

The most important thing to remember about the organization of meetings is that they should occur in mutually convenient surroundings where the most comfortable situations for conversation occur. The posture of openness on the part of the facilitator will make it possible to establish a personal relationship which makes this type of process work. Sit in a face-to-face position in an open posture throughout the meeting. Use the questioning technique to gain information and to clarify the learner's position.

When the facilitator has used questions which enable an understanding of the learner's needs and interests as well as providing an opportunity for the learner to view and perhaps clarify these needs and interests, the process of interaction between the two should be discussed. This is important because each situation may require totally different forms of interaction. Frequency of meetings and the role of the facilitator in the meetings should be discussed and be clearly understood by both parties.

The facilitator may find it useful to have materials available for perusal during these meetings. Discretion is the most useful word to remember when engaged in the sharing of information. There is a very narrow distance between the provision of support and the intrusion of unwanted materials and information. Materials on a side table (see illustration) are preferable to handing materials over to a person, particularly in the early stages of the meetings.

Side Table With Resources

Learner

Facilitator

As the meetings progress, the level of comfort and understanding will also increase. This is when the facilitator should feel much freer in introducing thoughts, materials, etc. It is still important to remember that the primary responsibility for decision making lies with the learner. A sensitivity to the learner's needs is still a prime requirement for the determination of input at this stage.

The meetings during the middle stage of the process are often the most comfortable for the facilitator and the learner. The relationship has been established and actions are supportive and purposeful. These meetings seem to have both direction and purpose unlike the latter stages which may hold some uncertainty for the facilitator.

The latter stages of involvement may occur because the learner is in the process of completing the learning or it may be because the learner has outgrown the need for the facilitator. It is important to be clear about which of these is true because different facilitative actions should be based on the requirements of the situation.

If the learner is attempting to bring completion to the process, the facilitator can play a useful part in the experience through his or her responses as a reactor to summative comments on the part of the learner. These responses should be genuine in keeping with the quality of the relationship which has evolved during the meetings of the two parties.

If the learner simply wishes to move into a new aspect of the learning where the facilitator's expertise is no longer needed, then the facilitator should act according to his or her wishes. Remember that this is not necessarily a reflection on the relationship between the facilitator and learner. It normally reflects the result of a successful process where both parties have been able to play positive roles.

It may be appropriate for the facilitator to identify resource persons or materials to support learning which will continue after the facilitator's involvement ends. Lists of materials such as films, audiotapes, videotapes, books, articles, etc., and an indication of the location of resources will enable the learner to acquire the requisite additional materials for learning. This activity should be entered into with the same belief in the learner which has characterized the relationship to this stage.

SUMMARY COMMENTS

The rewards of this approach to learning are considerable for both parties to the process. The learner can develop a good sense of personal accomplishment and an excellent relationship with another person. The facilitator can share in the knowledge of the learner's accomplishment and know that a positive contribution was made during the learning process.

This model can be best used where a one-to-one relationship is required and the learner experiences uncertainty in relation to the specific nature of the content and process of learning. Rather than force the learner into a "mold" or pattern which may be unsuitable, this model will allow for maximum flexibility and appropriate levels of support.

A major disadvantage of this model for some learners may be found in its very flexibility. Some learners despair when faced with uncertainty. They need a plan. Avoid the use of this model where a planned approach to learning is needed by the learner or the content.

If one wishes to see the effectiveness of the general approach taken by this model, one needs only to look at the success of client-centered therapy over the years. This approach to psychotherapy has been successful while other humanistic approaches to psychotherapy have learned from both its theory and practice.

I suggest that you read Carl Rogers' book, *Freedom to Learn in the '80's*, for further information related to this model.

Notes

1. Bruce Joyce and Marsha Weil, *Models of Teaching*, 3rd ed. (Englewood Cliffs, N.J.: Prentice-Hall, 1986), pp. 141-158.

2. R.E.Y. Wickett, "Adult Learning and Spiritual Growth," *Religious Education* 75: 5 (July-August, 1980), pp. 452-461.

3. C.O. Houle, *The Design of Education* (San Francisco: Jossey-Bass, 1972), pp. 96-101.

4. For facilitation, see Carl R. Rogers, *Freedom to Learn in the 80's* (Columbus, Ohio: Charles E. Merrill, 1983). For counseling, one could consult Carl R. Rogers, *Client-Centered Therapy: Its Current Practice, Implications, and Theory* (Boston: Houghton Mifflin, 1965) or any one of a number of works in the area of counseling by this author.

5. Ibid., pp. 119-134.

6. Carl R. Rogers, *On Becoming a Person* (Boston: Houghton Mifflin, 1961), pp. 50-55. See also Wickett's comments in "Working with Middle Aged Adults," in *Handbook of Adult Religious Education*, ed. Nancy T. Foltz (Birmingham, Ala.: Religious Education Press, 1986), pp. 100-101.

7. Rogers refers to two types of questions in the section called "Becoming a Facilitator" (pp. 135-145) in this book. The first type refers to questions which the facilitator should ask him or herself. The second type refers to the careful use of the question to cause reflection and clarification. Please note that *Freedom to Learn in the '80's* is seen by Rogers as a thorough revision of his earlier work, *Freedom to Learn*.

8. R.A. Horowitz, "Psychological Effects of the 'Open Classroom'," *Review of Educational Research* 49 (1979), pp. 71-85.

9. H.J. Wallberg, D. Schiller, and G.D. Haertel, "The Quiet Revolution in Educational Research," *Kappan* 61 (1979), pp. 179-183.

10. Rogers, *Freedom to Learn for the '80's*, p. 160.

Chapter 13

The Learning Covenant

This model suggests the utilization of the learning contract within the context of adult religious education. It has been renamed
to illustrate the nature of its appropriateness within this context.
The learner develops and enters into a written, contractual form
of agreement with a facilitator in this model.

This is a very effective model for use in a one-to-one situation or with a
group of learners, especially when the learner or learners have a well-devel-
oped sense of need. This particular model involves an adaptation of the
learning contract of Malcolm Knowles as an alternative to the existing traditional models.[1] As this model can be used with individuals or groups, it
forms a bridge between these two sections of the book.

The learning contract model, as proposed originally by Knowles, has
been adapted for use in a wide variety of settings. Primary users of this
model include institutions of higher education and staff development programs
in business and industry.[2] Very extensive usage provides a clear testament to
educators' views of its effectiveness.

Stephen Brookfield has reviewed the literature on the utilization of the
learning contract in a variety of settings, including the area of religious education. This author indicates that learning contracts have emerged as the
major approach to self-directed learning in numerous content areas.[3]

The development of Knowles contract method occurred after the original research by Allen Tough concerning the self-education of adults and
self-directed learning had been published.[4] It is clear from a reading of
Knowles' books that this type of thinking about adult learning had influenced
the conceptualization and development of the contract.[5] It would be true to

state that the contract method was consistent with the basic principles of andragogy.

One important major finding in Tough's work involves the issue of "main planner" for the projects. The fact that most respondents in studies of adult learning projects preferred to be the main planner or decision maker for their learning caused considerable discussion among adult educators.[6] The role of the learner in decision making is critical to the Knowles' approach to contracting.

Another influence on Knowles' work which can be seen in his books on contracting is that of David Kolb.[7] Knowles clearly values concrete experience in relation to learning in both the principles of andragogy and his later book on learning contracts.[8] The effective learning covenant will utilize the concrete base of experience in relation to the learning process.

One thing the reader should be aware of at the beginning of this chapter is the adaptability of the learning covenant approach to utilization in both one-to-one and group settings. As you will see in the description of this proposed model, it is essentially a one-to-one approach. It is used in group settings by negotiating a series of individual covenants with each learner. I propose the use of learning partnerships to enhance this group approach, particularly where large groups are involved.

I have used the model in both individual and group situations with very positive results. This chapter will outline first the individual situation then the group approach. Figure 1 indicates how covenants can operate in the group context.

Figure 1:   **The Covenant (in a group)**

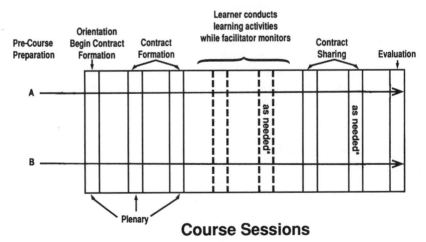

Course Sessions

* "As needed" refers to holding sessions as required
by learners and the demands of contracts.

There are certain preconditions which Knowles outlines for the success-ful use of this model. Unless these preconditions are met, it is difficult to imagine that the learning contract will achieve an acceptable result. The essence of Knowles' preconditions for the learners are:

1. A felt need to learn.
2. A supportive physical and psychological environment for the contract.
3. Learner identification with the goals of the learning contract.
4. Learner shared responsibility for planning and conducting the learning.
5. Active involvement by the learner in all parts of the learning process.
6. A connection between the learner's life experience and the learning pro-cess.
7. A feeling of some degree of success in progress toward the goals of the learning.[9]

The result of the meeting of these preconditions is a committed, involved, active learner with the maximum opportunity for success.

There is no doubt in my mind that many adult learners will meet the pre-conditions with ease. The greater challenge will be for the facilitator who must develop a relationship which enables the learner to take full advan-tage of his or her sense of commitment. The facilitator must be able to play a supportive role.

Stephen Brookfield states that forms of self-directed learning do not come easily to those who are accustomed to other methods.[10] This warning should be taken seriously by the facilitator of adult religious education. The initial reaction of many facilitators who are used to their role in the traditional for-mat is to be too directive in the planning and learning processes. A psy-chological shift is needed in order to enable rather than to control. A facil-itator must trust and believe in the learner's ability and desire to accomplish appropriate goals. The learner must also learn to be autonomous and self-directing as a learner, just as he or she is in other parts of life.

It is important to realize the potential value of this model for learning in the religious context. The first thing we should note is the high level of commitment which develops in the learning process. The contract also establishes a definitive framework within which the learning will occur. When the covenant has been achieved, both the learner and the facilitator know what to expect.

Another noteworthy point involves the use of the covenant in those situ-ations in which learner wishes to have a record of the accomplishment of learning. A covenant can provide clear evidence of accomplishment, thus meeting the individual's requirements for such evidence.

If a person wishes to increase the abilities and skills required for lay or other ministry, this is a particularly useful model for such development. I see this model as making its most valuable contribution in the acquisition of skills for ministry.

There are other forms of content which can be acquired quite effectively through this model. Although this model is most effective with skills, individuals may wish to acquire knowledge in relation to their religion. The study of scriptures, comparative religion, and other content may be learned in this manner.

We should be aware of the situations in which this model may not be useful. One situation in which it should be avoided would be the situation where flexibility in the planning and learning process is required. Some content does not lend itself to a clear and direct path for acquisition. Some learners prefer a more flexible approach which will allow for adjustments in goals and strategies.

A strong commitment to the covenant will emerge frequently which makes the learner feel that he or she must complete the requirements of the written document. Even an understanding and encouraging facilitator may have difficulty in convincing the learner to be more flexible if necessary.

Please note that the role of the facilitator frequently requires that patience should be exercised. The most important tool of the facilitator is the question, which can be used to open up new areas of thought or to clarify. It is important to remember that the purpose is to have the learner reach an understanding and to gain ownership of the ideas, etc. If this sense of ownership is not gained, many benefits of this model will be lost.

Another factor to be considered is the frequent desire of the learner to want to learn too much in any covenant. Perhaps it is the opportunity to be free to choose or the promised access to resources which causes this phenomenon. The problem is that too great a commitment with insufficient time and resources will lead to a sense of frustration and failure.

METHODOLOGY

It is crucial that the facilitator focus on the needs of the learner during the initial stage of the process. This means the provision of an appropriate, comfortable environment for the learning process. It may also mean that the learner needs to become familiar with this particular model. Learners may become familiar with the model through introductory remarks by the facilitator or through various publications.

Malcolm Knowles suggests that students read Part 1 of his book, *Self-Directed Learning*, as a preparatory activity.[11] This earlier book provides the essential information in fewer pages than the later volume. I suggest that learners should examine also the sample contract on pages 62-63 of the 1975 book, although alternatives could be found in the 1986 edition. This 1986 volume is a useful but lengthier option for the learners' preparation.

Example covenants which have been used in your particular setting will be helpful to prospective learners with no experience of the model. Keep a few of the best examples or design a good example to share with learners. Their confidence will be boosted by a clearer knowledge of expectations.

Learners with a low literacy level should be given verbal introductions and discussion opportunities to provide an adequate orientation. Should a contract be appropriate for a person of a low level of literacy for other reasons, the written part of the documentation should be kept as simple as possible. The process of simple contract development should contribute to the development of a higher level of literacy for some learners.

When the student is familiar with and has given a commitment to participate in a covenant process, it is important to hold a meeting or meetings to assist the learner to identify his or her specific needs. If the area under discussion involves a skill or skills for lay ministry, the learner should become familiar with the level of skill required as well as his or her present level of skill.

Descriptions of tasks can assist people to gain an increased familiarity of the required situation. The learner's sense of the need to learn should be considered an essential part of this process. An honest and mutually agreed understanding of the need can be achieved by a shared evaluation of existing skill levels.

The purpose, goals, and specific objectives for the covenant should be drawn very directly from the previously noted need identification process. Statements about the purpose and goals should be reviewed in discussion initially, but final clarification may occur as a result of a draft written statement. When behavioral objectives are required, they should be utilized in this mode.

At this stage of the process, I suggest that the learner prepare a draft of the proposed covenant. A general sense of direction is important, but greater precision and clarity can be obtained through the writing process. All parts of the covenant can be included because the final document should include all key phases of the process. Figure 2 provides an example of a possible draft document.

Figure 2:

LearningProject: Developing Skills for Lay Ministry   Duration: 4 months

Learning Objectives	Learning Resources and Strategies	Criteria and Means of Validating Evidence
1. To develop skills in conducting church-related visits to elderly and infirm people.	Organize a biweekly roster of people to be visited who are hospitalized, bed-ridden, or in nursing homes.	Invite a supervisor to attend at least three visits and to rate me on my ability to a) communicate b) show concerns.

2. To enhance my understanding of types of care offered by the church.	a) Participate twice a month at centers which distribute free food and clothing. b) Organize a social event each month to welcome newcomers. c) Attend self-help groups sponsored by the church at least once a week.	Write a comprehensive description of services offered by the church. Discuss these services in light of the needs of those in the church community.
3. To develop skills as a facilitator at educational events.	Conduct and observe education activities such as Bible studies, Sunday school, teacher training classes.	At the end of at least three teaching sessions have participants rate the effectiveness of my teaching methods and behavior.
4. To increase my ability to conduct worship events.	a) Read information on the music and traditions of worship b) Participate in contemporary forms of worship.	Plan and conduct worship services bimonthly employing a variety of worship styles.
5. To gain skill in conducting the administrative function of the church.	a) Be present at and assist in a goal-setting workship. b) Assist in preparing the financial budget for the next fiscal year.	Request a supervisor to observe and comment on work done in the administration of church duties.

The initial effort of draft preparation is the beginning of acceptance of "ownership" of what is to be learned. Respect and the ability to enable will assist the facilitator in the provision of support for the student. It is my experience that students value both questions and comments about the draft. Comments of approval should be a part of the discussion as clarification and improvements are sought in order to enhance the changes for a successful covenant.

I suggest that educational jargon be avoided wherever possible. Ask what someone "wants to learn." Then suggest that they put what they have described as the specific thing they want to learn under the heading of "objectives."

One key feature of this stage of the process is the identification of the resources which will be required. It is quite appropriate to suggest that the learner examine a wide range of possibilities at this stage. Accessibility may be a factor in certain instances, thus there may be a need to maximize options in the face of busy schedules or of long waits for materials from outside agencies.

There is one clear advantage which one can find in the use of this model, the use of a wider range of resources. Learners should be encouraged to step beyond the "classroom," and the facilitator can work with others when all demands do not have to be met by the individual facilitator. I have found that outside resource persons can be most helpful in areas beyond the normally limited expertise of any facilitator.

One example of the type of resource person to be utilized might be seen in the situation of training a home visitor for the care of a sick or otherwise confined person. It would be most useful to discuss the skills required with a person who has such skills and is using them in the same ministry. The facilitator can hope to identify the appropriate person for this experience. This is equally true for the identification of nonhuman resources as well.

The process for interaction with the resources should follow an appropriate pattern. This may involve such activities as the reading of introductory material prior to the process of interviewing resource persons. A different pattern will emerge in each instance.

A timetable will assist the learner to keep everything in order and in the correct stage of learning. This timetable can be incorporated into the covenant in a way that indicates the completion of interaction with resources or of activities; for example:

1. October 12 - completion of the literature review
2. October 30 - completion of initial interviews.

I believe that this is useful, provided that the dates are realistic and determined by the learner. The learner will see progress or when he or she is falling behind in the process.

Target dates can be extremely useful to the facilitator in the monitoring stage. They provide concrete bench marks to be checked and, if necessary, renegotiated. Learners often have a high level of commitment to their own target dates.

The evaluation criteria for the covenant should be agreed in advance by both the learner and the facilitator. They should be written into the covenant by the learner and agreed to by the facilitator in order to insure compatibility of needs. These criteria will help the learner to have a sense of achievement, and the facilitator will want to give appropriate encouragement to support the sense of achievement at the right time and under the right circumstances.

A clear statement of goals and objectives will aid in the process of determining evaluation criteria. The learner must be satisfied, and if there are institutional or other requirements the facilitator must also be satisfied. In the latter case of institutional requirements the learner must be aware of these and incorporate them into the covenant.

The evidence which is assembled to indicate the completion of the covenant should be stated clearly in the covenant. The nature of this evidence will be determined in part by the nature of the contract itself. If there are accreditation requirements by an institution, these requirements should be considered in the statements about and assembling of the evidence. In the absence of accreditation requirements, the evidence should be consistent with the learner's need to bring closure to the learning process.

The finalization of the covenant should occur after an appropriate process of refinement has been completed. The covenant should be clear, appropriate, and workable. When these criteria for assessing the initial covenant are met, dates for meetings to monitor the contract and for final feedback should be determined between the two parties.

Individual meetings will allow the learner to receive ongoing support and to see progress. Target dates should be reviewed and issues discussed. These meetings do provide opportunities to provide any needed encouragement and support. The learning which occurs in these sessions is often most valuable.

The number of meetings will be determined by the covenant and the needs of the learner. Two or three sessions may be sufficient in many covenants, although I suggest that at least one meeting be held in any month-long period. Weekly or more frequent meetings may occur in situations where learners require more assistance or have a shorter time period for the overall process.

This monitoring period is the time when most facilitators who are accustomed to the traditional role feel that they are not doing enough for the learner. This may lead to a temptation to be highly directive in these monitoring sessions. Please remember that the primary purpose of the facilitator is to enable the learner to complete his or her commitments. It is not to be a content specialist. Some provision of new content which is to clarify or extend areas in progress or to open a new area of the contract is permissible. The primary focus of the monitoring sessions should be on the process of learning followed by the content.

Both the evidence for the completion of the covenant and the criteria for its evaluation have been stated in advance as a part of the written covenant. Learners should be encouraged to assemble the evidence as the process continues. An example of this might be that the evidence of the Objective Number 1 is assembled when the objective has been completed.

A learner will have a sense of completion when the documentation which is assembled meets the self-described criteria for objective assessment. The facilitator can assist in the process by the provision of positive, critical, and honest comments. Remember that others may have input into this process also. Any required input should be described in the original covenant.

GROUP COVENANT SITUATIONS

It is quite possible that there will be several people involved in covenant learning simultaneously in your program. A support group can provide much of value to those who approach this model for the first time.

The purpose of the group is to give additional support for each individual learner. Learners should not be forced to adapt to the group's interest in any way. Rather, the group should provide the atmosphere within which the individual will continue to pursue a covenant based upon individual needs and interests.

My approach to the use of this model in groups is to follow these steps:

1. Ask learners to review the model in advance by reading one of the assigned texts or other appropriate materials.
2. Ask learners to focus on their areas of interest in advance.
3. Use the first part of the first session to outline the model and to discuss its implications. Clarification may be needed at this time.
4. Use the second part of the first session to have learners identify particular areas of interest followed by potential resources. This can be done in smaller groups such as diads or triads followed by a plenary session.
5. I try to use "learning partners" as a way of supporting the learning. The partner's job is to offer support as needed to assist in the clarification and writing process at the initial stage and in the learning process as well.
6. Ask learners to prepare a "draft" for review in the second session. This can be presented before the whole group, if the group is not too large, or before the partner in the diad.
7. Learners take away suggestions from the "draft" session and are encouraged to incorporate them into a final draft to be approved at the next session.
8. Share final "drafts" and receive approval from the members of the group and the facilitator on an individualized basis. (I suggest that each learner bring in two copies each time a review is to occur, one for the facilitator and the learner's own copy.)
9. Completion of the covenant. Learners proceed to complete the requirements of the covenant. They will have access to both the facilitator and the learning partner for support.
10. Use monitoring sessions to discuss progress with both the partners at the same time. This will keep everyone up to date and assist in problem solving and changes.

11. Final Group Meetings in which the group meets to have each learner share the results of the learning covenants. This will bring closure to the experience.

See Figure 1, which appeared earlier in the chapter, for a diagrammatic overview of the process. Appropriate adult education procedures should be used to insure a proper climate and introductory experience. Group members can become familiar with their various areas of interest. This will assist in the creation of a support system which includes diads and, where necessary, triads.

When this is done as a workshop experience in a specific period of time; for example, a Saturday afternoon, diads and triads can be used for ongoing activities. I assist people to form these small groups by listing names and interests on the board and by requesting the group to help make connections (see Figure 3).

Figure 3:

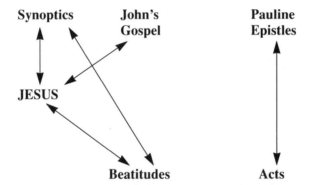

Once the covenant has reached the implementation stage, members of diads will often keep in touch to share information about resources and to ask questions about problems. This can be a valued addition to the support of the facilitator.

The sharing of the results of learning can be a very joyous occasion. It brings a sense of closure while also providing an additional opportunity for learning for all group members. The shared positive sense of accomplishment has made me realize the value of these sessions to those learners who tell me that they felt isolated in the prior experiences.

SUMMARY COMMENT

This model is most effective when there are specific objectives or "things" which the learner wants and needs to learn, particularly at his or her own pace.

It satisfies the requirement of a clear and precise plan or "curriculum" for learning while enabling the learner to participate in the plans formulation. Its greatest advantage may be found in the commitment of the learner which has been in evidence in so many situations where the model has been used.

The very specific nature of its plan may be its single most important disadvantage. Should a more open approach to learning be required, the learner may find both the content of the covenant difficult as well as the psychological commitment to complete the letter of the covenant.

There is little doubt of the effectiveness of this model based on the many years of application by adult religious educators and other followers of Malcolm Knowles. A perusal of the literature on learning contracts is bound to bring you to this conclusion.

The suggested reading for further exploration of this model includes two books by Malcolm Knowles, *Using Learning Contracts: Practical Approaches to Individualizing and Structuring Learning* and *Self-Directed Learning: A Guide for Learners and Teachers.*

Notes

1. Malcolm S. Knowles, *Self-Directed Learning: A Guide for Learners and Teachers* (Chicago: Follett, 1975) and *Using Learning Contracts: Practical Approaches to Individualizing and Structuring Learning* (San Francisco: Jossey-Bass, 1986).
2. Knowles, *Using Learning Contracts*, p. 42.
3. Stephen Brookfield, *Understanding and Facilitating Adult Learning* (San Francisco: Jossey-Bass, 1986), pp. 81-82.
4. Allen Tough, *Learning without a Teacher* (Toronto: The Ontario Institute for Studies in Education, 1975) and *The Adult's Learning Projects: A Fresh Approach to Theory and Practice in Adult Learning*, 2nd ed. (Toronto: The Ontario Institute for Studies in Education, 1971).
5. Knowles, *Using Learning Contracts*, pp. 28 and 40-41.
6. Many journals such as *Lifelong Learning* and *Adult Education* carried articles which commented on these issues, and conference papers presented at AEA meetings in the 1970s also reflected these discussions.
7. The most useful volume is David Kolb's book entitled *Experiential Learning: Experience as the Source of Learning and Development* (Englewood Cliffs, N.J.: Prentice-Hall, 1984).
8. Knowles, *Using Learning Contracts*, p. 1.
9. Ibid., pp. 7, 8.
10. Brookfield, *Understanding and Facilitating Adult Learning*, p. 82.
11. Knowles, *Self-Directed Learning*, p. 9.

Chapter 14

The Tip Of The Iceberg

The "Tip of the Iceberg" refers to the amount of learning which occurs in adult education classes as opposed to the larger base of the iceberg which is learning external to our classroom. Tough's model provides a vehicle for facilitating the learning we often do not see or recognize as important.

This model is based upon the method of facilitation practiced by Allen Tough in the Department of Adult Education at the Ontario Institute for Studies in Education. Like the other models, this one has been adapted to the context of adult religious education. It should be noted that the adaptation process was a relatively simple one in this instance. The model has been used for courses in "personal growth and change," thus it has been designed for a situation similar to that found in adult religious education.

My own experience with this model in the area of adult learning and development is that issues related to the spiritual or religious dimension of the person will arise on numerous occasions. The openness of this approach makes it a most appropriate vehicle for this type of learning.

Tough can be given much credit for our present emphasis on learning as opposed to teaching or education. The contribution of other authors such as Hartley Grattan[1] and Cyril Houle[2] to our thinking in this area had helped to prepare the adult educator to see beyond the limits of the "course," but Tough's research certainly propelled us forward in this aspect of learning.[3] We now know far more about the informal learning of adults.

To consider the major change which has occurred in the last two decades in the thinking of adult educators, we can cite the two major works of Malcolm Knowles, *The Modern Practice of Adult Education*[4] and *Self-*

Directed Learning: A Guide for Teachers and Learners.[5] The first book describes the traditional course model for adult education. Knowles' other book and subsequent recent publications, such as *Using Learning Contracts,*[6] clearly reflect the influence of Tough's emphasis on the importance of learner involvement in the decision-making process and individual learning activities.

The resulting change in Tough's personal approach to teaching has provided the basis for this model. My suggested changes in the model will hopefully allow it to be applied directly in adult religious educational settings.

This model is based upon a group situation where there is some flexibility in the overall content to be learned. It is possible to have a common element of content for all students in the group situation while also encouraging each student to pursue those individual interests which are related to the general content area outside of the classroom.

An example of where this model might work can be found in the area of scriptural studies. The general focus might be the New Testament. The group sessions might feature an overview of key aspects of the topic while individual learners would be encouraged to examine particular parts of the New Testament which were of interest to them.

Another example of where this model could be used would be in the exploration of issues of relevance to lifestyle and attitudes. The exposure to ideas in class can be combined with much reflection and other learning activities outside the class.

Tough developed this model because he saw the need to be flexible in the response to the needs of learners while providing some structure and the needed support for students' learning.[7] The flexibility is necessitated by the capacity for autonomous decision making on the part of adults which is related to their level of maturity and the search for satisfaction of a wide range of learning needs and interests.

A certain content area is selected for the group, thus providing some degree of security. The support for learners would include both the access to resources and other persons with whom discussions could take place. Tough sees both forms of support as helpful to learners.

I believe that the learning processes of certain types of content are aided by flexibility. An example of where this flexibility would be an asset would involve such things as values clarification and lifestyle-related issues. An investigative approach which enables the response to stimuli while moving in a general direction may prove fruitful for lifestyle-related areas of substantive content.

This model should not be applied where the content is rigid, narrow, or tightly defined by an outside party to the process. If the learner is required to follow a specific path to specific goals and objectives, this model should not be applied.

It should also be clear that this model will not work with learners who choose to be very dependent. Learners of this type who will not change should be encouraged to pursue more definitive models.

Tough indicates that this time spent outside of the group may be much more important in terms of the overall learning for many students.[8] He speaks of learning within the metaphor of the iceberg (see Figure 1).

Figure 1:

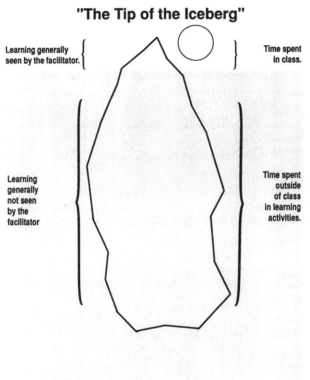

The iceberg is composed of two parts, one part above the water line and the other part below. The proportion of iceberg below the water line is always much greater than that above. The learning in the group or class is seen by the instructor and therefore is "above the water line." The learning outside the group in informal discussions, while reading or reflecting, and so on, is below the water line and generally unseen. This issue should not be exaggerated, but it should be considered carefully by the facilitator who wishes to maximize learning.

METHODOLOGY

Figure 2 provides an overview of this model and of the relationship between time spent inside and outside the group. We note the combined efforts within the group and the individual directions of the learners outside of the group meetings.

Figure 2:

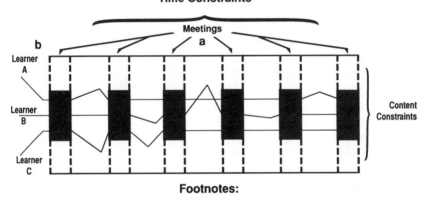

"The Tip of the Iceberg"

Time Constraints

Footnotes:

a:
Meetings contain common content
plus support for individual learning.
b:
Each learner enters with individual interests
and follows responsive, flexible path to learning.

A key factor in this model is the way we perceive the relationship between the time spent in the group and the total amount of learning which occurs for learners. The traditional point of view focuses upon the group as the most important part of the learning. The time spent outside of the group is seen to be tangential and relatively unimportant from this traditional perspective.

The planning for this course should be done in the context of an advisory committee with input to the planning process.[9] Course revisions should take into account the input from learners who should be asked to evaluate resource materials.[10]

Once the pre-course planning has been completed, the process should follow the outline of Figure 2. The steps would be as follows:

1. The pre-course planning occurs with a group of representative learners in cooperation with content specialists and facilitator.

2. The initial meeting of the group is designed to acquaint people with the model and its workings. Climate setting should be followed by process description and a review of resources (see chapter 7).

3. The first part of each subsequent meeting prior to the final stage will involve sharing of activities between sessions. This is a time for problem identification as well as sharing information about resources, and so on. This should last as long as is necessary without preempting too much of the time needed for the next part.

4. The middle stage of meetings should be devoted to sharing substantive content. The facilitator leads this stage.

5. The latter stage involves the identification of resource materials which may be needed by the learners in future activities.

6. The group meeting or meetings which occur toward the end should involve opportunities for more sharing by the students of the results of their learning process. This will increase the total knowledge of the group and bring a sense of completion to the process.

7. The student should be encouraged to synthesize the results of the learning process in some way, either through a paper or discussion.

The role of the facilitator is critical in this model. He or she must provide content information, stimulation, and support. The role in this model combines the talents of a traditional adult educator with those talents which we associate with the facilitation of self-directed learning.

Substantive content is to be provided in group meetings or classes during one portion of the total time available. Somewhat traditional ways of providing knowledge and skills in interesting and stimulating ways will be used in the middle portion of each session. Traditional climate setting exercises which involve familiarization with learners and their interests and "wants" are utilized in the earliest sessions to determine certain aspects of content which will be included or will receive more emphasis in later sessions.

Learners will be introduced to a common set of resources brought in by the facilitator in a cardboard "box" or similar convenient manner. This enables the learners to discover and share a common set of resources which are most conveniently provided in one in-class location. (I have found that learners often appreciate this very much.)

The reading list and "box" will stimulate and support outside activities to a greater extent than if learners had to spend hours searching through libraries and other sources of information. New items found to be helpful can be added to the box or list by either the facilitator or the learners. A facilitator can begin the process and encourage others to follow. The process of addition can be enhanced by the facilitator's increased understanding of the items which would most suit each particular need and interest. Learners can be encouraged to add materials based upon what helped them and what may be of assistance to others. Anyone who adds anything should be encouraged to comment on its addition. I request that people sign items out and return them each week. Only when others have had the opportunity to borrow them will a second chance be provided for further study.

After the initial meeting of introductions and climate setting, learners should be encouraged through resource suggestions and other means to pursue their own learning paths. If the course is for credit, this may involve assurances that their learning will be accredited. The facilitator should encourage individuality and flexibility as well as provide information and stimulation.

The opening part of each new meeting should involve a period of getting in touch with the various individual activities. Asking people to share anything interesting they have read or done is a useful approach. Even disappointments and negative views may be shared about books or inaccessible resources. There may be solutions to resource problems which are identified by anyone. This process will assist the facilitator to keep in touch with the previously unseen part of the "iceberg" of learning.

The second part of each meeting should be devoted to new content. The process may vary but should conform to good adult education practice. This approach will insure that the common content of the course is considered, understood, and integrated into the overall process in an appropriate manner.

The latter stages of each meeting should be devoted to the identification of resources for future learning. This would include the potential resources which might be used to pursue learning which emerged from the session's activities. It might also include the identification of further resources which did not come to mind during the discussion of individual learner's activities in the first part of the session or which are part of the general content of the course.

As the final meetings of the group begin, it is useful to bring some sense of accomplishment to this part of the learning process. It would be inaccurate to suggest that this would be the end of the process for all learners in the group. Future learning may occur and resources should be identified where possible to support the continuous learning of any individual. The intention is to give the learner some sense of progress, and the support which a positive experience normally brings, to encourage continuous activity. Opportunities for sharing the results of one's learning verbally should occur in fifteen to thirty minute segments.

The facilitator in this model can achieve a type of "split personality" in the performance of his/her role in three distinct parts of the process in each group session. These periods of review, content delivery, and preparation for future learning can be planned carefully to insure that all areas of responsibility are covered. Spontaneity will emerge with experience. The learners will create their own dynamic process when given permission and support along with good content. I have found that the final phases of the course have more learner control and input which often blurs the need to have three clear sections.

SUMMARY COMMENTS

The learner who is committed to some group participation because he or she values discussion and access to resources while wanting some individuality in the learning process will value this model. It has all the positive features of informed leadership, discussion opportunities, stimulating content delivery, and the individual activity outside the group which is valued. I think that it is particularly valuable for learners who feel they need the security of some knowledgeable "instructor" and some content delivery while pursuing individual goals.

I have doubts about the use of this model in a situation where maximum flexibility or individual attention is required. There are also situations where a learning plan encompassing all types of learning, both inside and outside the group or class, is more effective. Learners may not find it easy to cope with the flexibility of non-group time.

This model may not work effectively where there is a considerable amount of common content which must be learned by all participants inside and outside the group sessions. It will not replace the models where individual attention is a requirement, thus it should not be used in place of the one-to-one models.

I recommend that further investigation of this model be pursued by viewing the previously cited videotape, "The Tip of the Iceberg," and reading pages 131 to 133 in the previously cited book, *Intentional Changes: A Fresh Approach to Helping People Change*.

Notes

1. C. Hartley Grattan, I*n Quest of Knowledge: A Historical Perspective on Adult Education* (New York: Association Press, 1955), p. 3.

2. Cyril O. Houle, *The Design of Education* (San Francisco: Jossey-Bass, 1972); Cyril O. Houle, *Continuing Learning in the Professions* (San Francisco: Jossey-Bass, 1981); and C.O. Houle, *Patterns of Learning* (San Francisco: Jossey-Bass, 1984).

3. Allen Tough, *The Adult's Learning Projects: A Fresh Approach to Theory and*

Practice in Adult Learning, 2nd ed. (Toronto: The Ontario Institute for Studies in Education, 1979).

4. Malcolm S. Knowles, *The Modern Practice of Adult Education: From Pedagogy to Andragogy*, rev. ed. (Chicago: Follett, 1980). The earlier edition was published in 1970.

5. Malcolm S. Knowles, *Self-Directed Learning: A Guide for Learners and Teachers* (Chicago: Follett, 1986).

6. Malcolm S. Knowles, *Using Learning Contracts: Practical Approaches to Individualizing and Structuring Learning* (San Francisco: Jossey-Bass, 1986).

7. Allen Tough, *Intentional Changes: A Fresh Approach to Helping People Change* (Chicago: Follett, 1982), pp. 132-133.

8. See Tough's comments on this issue in the videotape, "The Tip of the Iceberg," which is part of the package entitled *The Design of Self-Directed Learning*, with Allen Tough, Virginia Griffin, Bill Barnard, and Don Brundage. The package was edited by Reg. Herman and published by the Ontario Institute for Studies in Education and Ryerson Polytechnic Institute, Toronto, Canada.

9. This is a deviation from Tough's original approach where the course is planned and changes are made in future courses based upon student input. See *Intentional Changes*, p. 132.

10. Ibid.

Chapter 15

The Interdependent Group

Working together in an equal manner is achieved through mutual respect and commitment to learning. This model helps people work together to achieve their individual goals in a supportive structure. The facilitator helps the learners to identify goals and resources in a process of cooperation stressed to enable the achievement of desired goals. The process interweaves classroom discussions and external activities of a cooperative nature to maximize growth and learning.

This model represents an adaptation of an approach to teaching and learning developed and used by Virginia Griffin in her courses which concern the facilitation of adult learning.[1] It is a model which combines some of the best features of self-direction with the advantages of group support. Other models may emphasize the advantages of self-direction to the extent that there is a higher level of individual activity than is considered desirable. Most traditional models focus attention more directly on the shared interests or needs. This model involves group and individual activities in a manner which insures that individual needs will not be neglected. David Boud would see this model as including elements of both self-direction and learner-centered education.[2]

The model is referred to as an "interdependent" model because it emphasizes working relationships with members of a group. Each learner is dependent on other learners for mutual support in the learning process. The support is provided to insure the accomplishment of goals and the successful completion of learning. Individual goals are more easily achieved in certain circumstances through the support of groups.

The exciting aspect of this model is that it moves the learner away from dependence on authority while not isolating the learner in the final process. The balance between the two possible extremes is found in interdependence. We can move toward this position, although Gwynneth Griffith suggests that we never fully achieve it.[3]

Griffith describes an important transition in the teaching/learning process in moving from dependence to interdependence. Dependency assumes the teacher's role as expert and the learner as repository of new substantive content while interdependence assumes the teacher and learner combine their roles interchangeably as expert and learner.[4] Independence on the part of the learner assumes in Griffith's view that the learner is self-directed and the teacher is a mere resource for the learner.[5]

The programs for learning at the Centre for Christian Studies in Toronto and elsewhere which incorporate this approach have indicated that this model provides a very positive alternative to the traditional models of teaching adults.[6] At the very heart of this model is the belief in self-direction. Learners are expected to participate fully in both the planning of class activities and all other relevant sub-group and individual activities. This model combines the three levels of activity in ways appropriate to each learner in order to achieve the desired results.

One can readily visualize a number of situations in which this model will be workable for adult Christian education. A group of learners may wish to examine various aspects of an issue, or a group concerned with sacred scriptures may have several different but interrelated foci. If you can remember a situation where you know that several people wanted to learn about different but related topics, all of which involved different aspects of a larger topic such as the New Testament or some other major component of religion, you will know where this model may be used. This model makes it possible to pursue each interest while continuing to have the group input and support.

It should be noted that Griffin has used this approach very effectively to enhance the learners' abilities in self-direction. A learner who has doubts or concerns about his or her ability to accomplish chosen goals or objectives can be assisted to see the possibilities for learning and be made more aware and able through the process. The presence of a sensitive facilitator will make this possible.

Virginia Griffin has noted that many learners experienced a transformation in her courses which enabled them to be more self-directed. This involved a perspective transformation which Griffin compares to the difference between sitting in the back seat of a car and sitting in the driver's seat where one is in control.[7] The analogy is most apt and applies to different aspects of one's perspective on the teacher and one's peers. This transformation of perspective toward the teacher is quite critical. To cease to view the teacher as a superior being and the fount of all that is good and useful is most difficult for those who have been taught to revere teachers or, indeed, any person with expertise. Any teacher knows that he or she has limitations, although each one of us does have special expertise. That is why we have been chosen to do the job. Perhaps we need to remember the virtue of humility.

A critical feature in this process is the manner in which the learner becomes transformed. The learner begins to see his or her own resources such as previously acquired knowledge and skills as having value. The learner will begin to understand that, in the final analysis, he or she is the person who must be satisfied with the results of the learning activity.

It is clear that the most important change for many learners who participate in courses using this model is in the area of attitudes. The transformation can affect the way we view the learners who are participating in a process beside us. It is now possible to become more aware of the contributions others bring to the situation. We know that adults normally bring considerable experience to the classroom. Often that experience is based on an aspect of the content of the class. Perhaps they have engaged in a considerable amount of learning in the content area in a recent learning project. Learners are far more likely to discover each other's potential contribution in an interdependent group.[8]

Knowledge is also affected in the transformation from other-directed to self-directed learning in the classroom. Learners become more aware of what they have learned as a separate and distinct form of knowledge or understanding. This would be the acquired, integrated knowledge most relevant to the individual's learning needs.

In fact, adults frequently acquire a new knowledge based upon a combination of their needs, interests, and prior experience. Learners take what they want in the learning process based upon their situation. Unless we have a sound reason to do otherwise, we should accept the validity of this knowledge to the individual who possesses it.

This phenomenon can be seen quite readily in certain skill areas. It is clear in many groups that different levels of skills are acquired even when all participants have been given the same opportunity to learn exactly the same skill at the same level. Perhaps ability is not the only factor in determining the level of achievement. Needs and interests may play a major role in determining exactly what type of attitude, skill, or knowledge will be acquired.

The fact is that the learner need no longer seek external approval for all that has been learned. Knowledge or skill that is seen to have value to the learner is the primary basis for satisfaction.[9]

METHODOLOGY

The series of steps followed in this class can be summarized as follows:

1. Climate setting to insure the development of openness and good working relationships.
2. An in-depth review of student's interests (which may take a considerable period of time for exploration).
3. Decisions about areas of focus for learning and development of relationships with learning partners.
4. Partners proceed to work together with returns to the plenary at appropriate intervals.
5. Learners share the results of their learning activities with the plenary.
6. Evaluation and closure occurs.

Figure 1 provides an overview of this process.

Figure 1:

The Interdependant Group

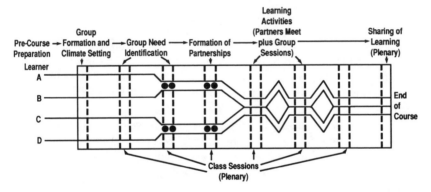

This class follows the general approach of determining individual and group needs in the initial stages. Climate setting is crucial in this approach, and particular attention should be paid to the relationships which develop among group members. The facilitator should use large sheets of newsprint which can be taped together onto a large surface or board. The newsprint is better than a board which does not hold a permanent record because it allows the responses to be recorded once and returned to subsequent sessions for further review and change. Interests and needs should be recorded systematically on the large sheets of newsprint.

Middle stages in the series of class meetings can be held to provide support for longer term sub-group learning activities as well as for short-term learning reports from sub-groups or individuals. It is often useful to divide the larger group into the sub-groups during class time to enable the members to continue their activities.

The latter stages of the course will provide the opportunity for culminating activities which help to bring closure to the learning activities of the class and its members. It is important to bring the class sessions to some form of closure while continuing to maintain the options for future learning.

The role of the facilitator in the early part of the class is to bring the level of comfort and awareness to the appropriate points. Learners may need the security which provides a basis for the transformation process. It is also true to say that the expertise of the facilitator in the clarification and resource identification is critical.

The facilitator should arrange the initial class sessions into a circular format with a good view of a large surface for recording comments. See Figure 2 for a description of the arrangements. The facilitator will normally record the results of the discussion.

Figure 2:   **Newsprint**

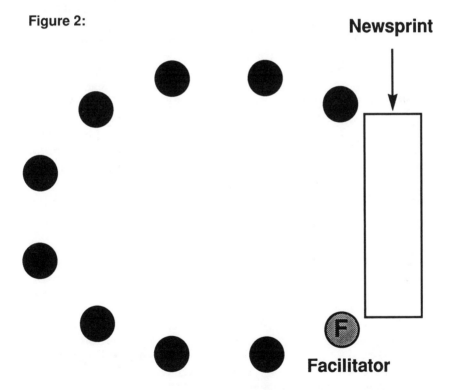

Facilitator

The initial discussions will assist learners to discover the linkages between or among their various interests. It appears to be most effective when the linkages are made visually on a board, and the learners identify both their interests and the potential linkages as part of the process. Figure 3 provides an example of the ways in which this type of recording may occur.

Figure 3:

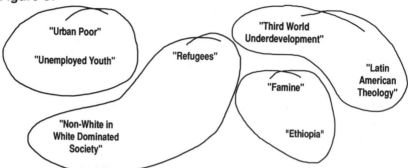

As you can see, the linkages may be very natural or quite indirect. There may also be situations in which students do have quite individual needs which must be considered. This does not necessarily mean that the group will not be able to participate in the supporting activities in relation to the learning. Previous learning on the part of peers may be utilized to provide much needed information.

The best format for creating the correct situation for communication would be one in which the students assemble in a circle for the plenary sessions with the facilitator and board on one side. When it is appropriate to create sub-groups in the initial stages, the situation will normally involve diads or triads. These smaller groups should be placed in chairs in full view of the board which contains their ideas, interests, and needs (see Figure 4).

Figure 4:

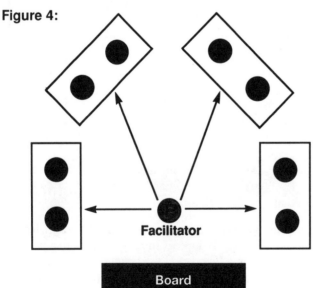

There are a number of reasons why I suggest we follow this particular format. It is important that the individual learner's interests
be visible reminders at all times to the group process. These are the
items which caused the learners to want to participate in this learning group rather than any other group. Also, we need to remember
that the groups must always be aware they exist to enable individuals to meet their needs. The interdependent groups are not required
to seek consensus-based learning goals. They should not be tempted to move in that direction. Rather than moving together all of the
time, they should be seeking ways to support each others' learning
goals.

Sub-groups may meet within the format of the total group's meetings
or they may wish to hold meetings quite separately. Additional separate
meetings may be required along with other forms of sub-group activities in libraries or in interviews or in other learning situations. The key is
for the facilitator to encourage and support any relevant activity the sub-
group may wish to follow.

I suggest the following procedure as appropriate. After the initial climate setting exercises which allow for later interaction, utilize some
form of individual consideration of needs and interests. Have the individual record these interests and needs through a nominal group process. They should be well established in the person's mind prior to group
involvement on content issues. These items should then be recorded and
organized into the sub-groupings as recognized by the facilitator and the
learners.

As learners begin to engage in activities in sub-groups, the plenary
sessions become communication-oriented in terms of the result of sub-
group activities. Plenary meetings provide the opportunity for sharing
difficulties or questions as well as the results of the sub-groups' work.

Each sub-group and individual should be supported in the process of
sharing the results of their activities with the plenary. This increases the
overall learning of the group while enabling individuals and sub-groups
to engage in the reinforcement of learning which normally occurs in the
process of planning and preparing presentations.

The process of sharing will assist the members of sub-groups and individual learners to share the results of their activities with learners who are
interested in related areas. The benefits to both parties are considerable.
Those who provide the new information or skill will have an increased
sense of accomplishment through the process. New interests may come to
the fore as other learners provide a new perspective for those who have
been working on different topics. Those learners who have been working
in another aspect of the same topic will find their knowledge or skills
are expanded through the results of others' learning.

SUMMARY COMMENTS

When this model is properly applied it provides many of the advantages which accrue from group sessions while also providing the very high level of individual decision making. It is through this emphasis on the learner's role in which the value of the learner is recognized that the transformation between the other-directed and the self-directed learner will begin to occur.

This model may be used to assist learners to change their approach to learning from other-directed to self-directed. Its greatest advantages can be found in the respect for the learner and the learner's role in the learning process which it engenders.

The model should not be used by those who experience frustration in the process of planning their own learning along with the learning of others. Avoid use of this model where learners are required to learn something in some particular way. A meaningless process of participation normally results from the manipulation of learners into situations they would not otherwise choose to be in.

Virginia Griffin has been using the original model on which my suggestions are based for several years. The students in her groups have found it to be a most rewarding experience on a personal level. Many former students have used it in their own practice.

Further information about this model may be found in the book, *Learning Partnerships: Interdependent Learning in Adult Education*, particularly the chapter by Gwynneth Griffith entitled "Images of Interdependence: Authority and Power in Teaching/Learning," and the portions of the tapes from the previously mentioned series, *The Design of Self-Directed Learning*, in which Virginia Griffin appears.

Notes

1. Virginia Griffin is a member of the faculty of the Department of Adult Education at the Ontario Institute for Studies in Education, Toronto, Canada. This statement is based on personal communication with this educator and author in July of 1989.

2. David Boud, "A Facilitator's View of Adult Learning," in *Appreciating Adults Learning: From the Learners' Perspective*, ed. David Boud and Virginia Griffin (London: Kogan Page, 1987), pp. 224-226.

3. Gwynneth Griffith, "Images of Interdependence: Authority and Power in Teaching/Learning," in *Appreciating Adults Learning: From the Learners' Perspective*, ed. David Boud and Virginia Griffin (London: Kogan Page, 1987), p. 57.

4. Ibid., p. 60.

5. Ibid.

6. Ibid., pp. 51-63.

7. See the videotape, "Learning Transitions," with Virginia Griffin in *The Design of Self-Directed Learning*, edited by Reg. Herman and produced by the Ontario

Institute for Studies in Education and Ryerson Polytechnical Institute, Toronto, 1980.

8. Joan Robertson, Sharon Saberton, and Virginia Griffin, *Learning Partnerships: Interdependent Learning in Adult Education* (Toronto: Department of Adult Education, Ontario Institute for Studies in Education, July, 1985).

9. See Virginia Griffin in the videotape, "Learning Transitions."

Chapter 16

The Study Circle

Study Circles involve formal groups of adults in a democrati-
cally directed learning process with the assistance of a facilitator.
There is no teacher nor is there a prepackaged program which students are required to follow. The model has been used extensively in churches and other settings.

    The Scandinavians have provided us with a helpful model for adult learn-
er involvement in the process of group learning. It is a model which has
been utilized in a variety of settings including churches and other religious
groups. Its very origins come from the result of the work of a prominent
church leader and educator of the previous century. It has been developed and
refined through folk schools, labor unions, and other institutions in Europe
as well as in the church.[1]
    N.F.S. Grundtwig of Denmark has a well-deserved reputation for his
leadership role in the field of adult education.[2] This nineteenth-century cler-
ic and other Scandinavian educators set the stage for this region's emergence as a world leader in innovative adult education practice. Folk schools
and study circles emerged from these countries as a result of the development
of Scandinavian adult education, thus providing many other countries with
examples and inspiration.[3]
    A recent article by Clay Warren comments on the links between andragogy
and the work of Grundtwig based on the views of the influential adult educator, Eduard Lindeman.[4] There are several ways we can see the linkage
between the assumptions of andragogy, as expressed by Lindeman and
Knowles, and those of Grundtwig. Both sets of assumptions regard "sub-

ject" centered learning as less important for adults. They also agree on the importance of life experience.[5]

In recent years, Sweden has been particularly influential in our thinking about this model. Leonard Oliver has provided us with a most useful review of the Swedish activities of recent years and an American view of the value of this model.[6]

If representations could be made in either one-to-one models or group models of adult education in terms of levels of self-direction and facilitative support, this method represents a very high level of learner direction and of supportive facilitation. It should be noted that the facilitator in this group is not expected to be a resource person. The facilitator is considered to be solely a process person in this model.

This model has considerable merit as a model for social action and community-building activity.[7] The involvement of people in a democratic process of decision making through the consideration of all possibilities and the assumption of responsibility through votes and the division of support activity is a firm base for collective decision making. It is true, nevertheless, that there is considerable individual learning in this model, thus making it a good bridge between these two sections of the book.

This model will be most appropriate for adult religious education situations where a sense of group cohesion is important. If you are faced with a situation in which either group solidarity or social action is your church's goal, this model will help you meet these goals.

Another factor to be considered is the nature of the background of the potential members of the study circle. When people have a desire to be involved in a group which is not teacher-directed and to have access to resource persons other than the teacher to provide what is required, this model will work well.

Participation in study circles is a purely volunteer action. Those persons who choose to be involved in study circles do so because of common interests in learning and a shared commitment to learn in the democratic model. The model will not work well when there is no commitment to the democratic process or where the expectation of other-directed learning is wanted or required. The tremendous potential of a group is unleashed in this model because all members are encouraged to participate in all aspects of the learning process. Like the other group models, learners begin to develop a greater respect for self and fellow learners while sharing.

One must think in quite different ways in order to make the model work effectively. The following points are essential to its operation:

1. The study circle is not a class.
2. Learners are not students in the traditional manner.

3. There are no formal credit or prerequisites involved in the study circle model.
4. The study circle is life centered.
5. There is no teacher.[8]

I cannot stress the last point sufficiently. The uniqueness of this model in relation to the traditional model clearly stems from the total absence of the teacher. The adjustments which are made and the opportunities which are presented by this situation do provide us with a quite different situation. When the group has adjusted to this and the other factors and to the logical consequences which follow, it is possible to proceed with the study circle.

Study circles work best when the membership is comprised of five to twenty members who attend the sessions along with the facilitator or leader.[9] There should be a trained leader at each session in order to insure that the process is followed in an appropriate manner. It is also important to have a plan which has been determined and is to be followed by the group.

It should be noted that the leader and his or her actions must be sanctioned by the group. There is a sense in which the role of leader is like that of the chair of a meeting or committee. It is a "service" role rather than a directive role. The ultimate authority in all situations resides with the group and its collective decision-making process.

METHODOLOGY

The study circle is based on common interests in learning and a commitment to participate in the learning process in a fully involved, democratic fashion. Learners will meet together with the guidance of a leader or facilitator to explore their interests. The purpose of the initial session will be to confirm this interest and approach to meeting learner needs.

The following points outline the basic process of our model:

1. Advance information is shared with all potential participants. All members of the community must receive it.
2. The formation of the study circle occurs in the initial meeting as people become aware of its purpose and methods.
3. Participants share ideas and interest within the general context of the circle's purpose.
4. Discussions occur to enable clarification of ideas and interests and the role which the study circle can play for the group and its members.

5. The group determines its plan of action by democratic decision making. The facilitator is an equal member.
6. The resources and data are gathered and shared within the group.
7. Plans can be changed and developed through mutual agreement in a democratic fashion.
8. The group evaluates its own process of learning.

These steps provide a basis for the circle's process. Figure 1 provides a visual overview of the process.

Figure 1:

The Study Circle

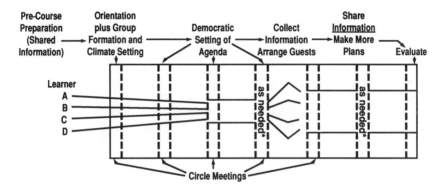

* "As needed" refers to the holding of meetings as required.

The best physical arrangement for the organization of a study circle is the formation in which no individual has prominence over any other in the seating arrangements (see Figure 2). This is particularly important in the placement of a leader. It is all too easy for our facilitator to assume unconsciously (or consciously) a position of prominence in the group. To do so in this situation will defeat the purpose of the method and return us to an alternative method which was not selected for use.

This initial meeting will require special planning in a context where the participants are not accustomed to the study circle method. The leader will want to spend time insuring that the learners understand the nature of the process of the group and of their roles in the new situation.

One method which has been used to acquaint people more fully with the process in the first session is to have people share information about their knowledge of study circles and their expectations of the process in the initial

Figure 2:

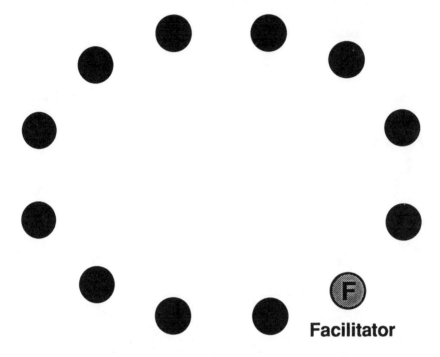

Facilitator

part of the session. Several people could be given specific information on pieces of paper which they are requested to share at the appropriate moments. These pieces should be given to those persons before the meeting in order that they can seek clarification or further information about their part in the sharing process.

The material to be distributed in advance could include a brief description of the nature of the democratic process and the roles of learners and leaders. Other items could be shared and discussed before further activity is planned. This will enable the group members to learn about study circles in a manner consistent with the basic approach of the model.

When all members of the group have a basic understanding of the principles the initial process of the study circle should begin. The initial planning of the group will begin with clarification of ideas and issues based on statements by all members of needs and interests.

The leader has a critical role in the process at this stage. It is the leader's responsibility to insure participation by the learners at the times in the process when it is appropriate to do so. The initial stages are certainly a point where all learners need to be involved in order to insure that their interests and needs are considered in the critical planning phase.

The selection of a leader may be through an election by the group, or a leader may be selected in advance prior to the group's assembly. In either case, the leader should be sufficiently knowledgeable and skilled in study circle methodology to insure that the group will function according to the basic principles of the method.

The leader will be responsible for the acquisition of resource materials for the group from time to time. As a representative of the sponsoring agency, the leader will obtain resources which may be supplied by that sponsoring agency. If guest resource persons are to attend meetings of the study circle, the leader may extend the invitation and explain the nature of the circle and its requirements to any guest.

Each member of the study circle must be prepared to accept responsibility for the learning which is to occur in the meetings. This is part of the reason why it is so important to encourage the input of all members and the use of the democratic process. This will mean that members of the circle will need to engage in activity outside of meeting times such as searching out information or contact resources to bring that which is needed back to the group.

There is an advantage in keeping a record of decisions made by the group. Since decisions often require action on the part of group members, members may wish to appoint a recorder. It would be preferable to have this power vested in a person other than the leader or facilitator in order to avoid the centrality of responsibility which this dual role would imply. Please note that the democratic process may continue to apply throughout the series of meetings of the study circle. A change in direction of the plan should involve a group discussion and a sense of commitment as expressed by the membership.

This factor may hinder flexibility at times. The group may not be prepared to change plans in spite of the wish of a few members. The advantage is that the members must learn how to work together and to solve the problems based on any differences.

One of the things I have noted as the members of the study circle engage in a successful experience is that they grow in confidence. The ability to be in control while accomplishing common goals provides very positive reactions as in other learner directed models.

After the initial phase which involved the building of the members into a working group and the establishment of a plan for learning, the leader and members will need to proceed to complete the requirements of the plan. Resource persons will be contacted, and the gathering of information will begin. The leader and members of the circle should be prepared to provide brief progress reports of their actions during regular sessions. This will enable problems to be solved through collective thought and the requisite actions.

The plan should call for the appropriate spacing of information sharing and external resource persons' interventions into the circle. The outline of a plan included in Example 1 provides an indication of the type of plan which might emerge from a meeting.

Example 1

(Please note: This example uses a Christian context because I do not feel able to do justice to a non-Christian context. I trust that the reader will forgive my limitations.)

1. The meeting of the group is advertised with a clear indication of the content area in general and of the nature of the process.

This group has chosen to meet under the general title of "The Social Message of the Gospels." It was a relatively appropriate title because members of the group had become concerned about the way they could live out the message of the gospels in a troubled society.

2. The group gathers together to become acquainted with each other and, if necessary, the study circle methodology. (I have used a specific method to do this where several members of the group receive a piece of paper with a "fact" about study circles which they can share with the group.)

Many members of the group know each other, but a few new people have come along out of curiosity and interest in the potential direction of a church group with social concerns. They have been reassured that this is a new situation for learning where the planning will be done together. Individuals share their knowledge and perspectives of the new model.

3. The group needs to begin the organizational process. This is accomplished by having people share their interests and ideas. The accumulation of these ideas and interests will give a basis for future decisions.

Members of the group began to express their concerns about some negative situations in their immediate communities and beyond. Unemployment, particularly among young people, is noted. The list goes on to include racism, Third World debts and Third World underdevelopment, plus poverty in the inner city. The questions are raised in such a way that some people are uncertain as to the connection between these problems and the gospels.

4. The group determines the content to be covered in the meetings. This may stretch the boundaries of the original title at times. Such flexibility is quite appropriate in many instances.

5. The group organizes its meetings and determines the resources needed. The facilitator will obtain needed external resources (human and nonhuman).

A second meeting is held to continue the exploration of specific topics to be covered in future meetings. The facilitator and others have sought to uncover possible resource materials and persons for the group to consider, should they wish to do so. At this second meeting, people begin to decide on topics for the next three meetings. One guest speaker will be invited while four members of the group agree to review materials provided by the facilitator and from other sources and to report back to the circle. Other topics will be chosen as the need arises. The initial topic is "poverty in our own community and beyond."

6. Meetings occur after the schedule has been agreed on and the initial resources have been obtained. The group will continue to meet to complete the process.

Our circle meets with the representative of a local church committee which is involved in sharing food and clothing with people in need, including younger and older persons and families. This person describes the way the committee believes that it is acting out the message which it sees contained in the gospels about how Christians should respond to the poor. Other committee members share their views as a result of interviews with other church agencies, readings, and visits to see relevant activities. The circle decides it must do more to explore the response of their faith community to this situation in their secular community.

7. Evaluative statements will be welcome in order to keep the group process consistent with the needs of the learners.

Some group members express a concern during the meetings that more issues need to be considered. There is an attempt to include sessions after the initial exploration of poverty through the provision of time to discuss topics which the circle feels should be included. A combination of external and internal persons is sought in order to have some time on each topic.

8. A final evaluative process will begin after the learning process has been otherwise completed. This will enable the group to obtain closure on one process and to move to the next opportunity.
   The group decides that this circle must continue to meet to explore action plans to implement in the faith community. The learning has been useful, but there is a feeling that the process will be incomplete without some action to

change the faith community to be more consistent with the gospel message.

This plan illustrates the possible spacing and organization which might occur. External resource persons are used at as early a point as possible while members are given time to work on the collection of content which is to be shared.

The meetings will proceed with input from selected resource persons and group members who have undertaken certain responsibilities to obtain and share information. The input should be provided in such a way that maximum discussion rather than one-way communication is encouraged.

Material resources should be shared with the group members in a manner which provides accessibility to all who wish it. The leader or other member who acquires the material for the group should make certain that sufficient copies or adequate circulation procedures occur for the benefit of the complete circle.

It is appropriate for the study circle to review its own activities and to evaluate its own activities. The leader should assist in this process according to the circle's wishes in this area. Such procedures will enable the circle to gain a sense of accomplishment and to learn how to work more effectively in the future.

SUMMARY COMMENTS

This is an effective model that has been tried in the context of the type of adult religious learning which is the focus for this book. We can be grateful to the Scandinavian churches and others who did such an excellent job to develop it.

The advantages of the model can be found in its ability to treat learners as equals in a democratic process aimed at learning. It will promote a sense of the group and provide a vehicle for social action. Both individual learning and group learning will be enhanced by this model.

The model should definitely be avoided in situations where the type of learning required is individual in nature or where learners are unhappy with democratic processes in the classroom. The individual learner may be frustrated by a group which has other priorities than his or her own. It is not always possible to accommodate everyone all the time in groups, thus leading to other choices for such situations where individualization is demanded by the learner or the particular content to be learned.

The advantages of the model are the clear promotion of community learning and growth. The will to change will be strengthened by the interactions created by the model. Its disadvantages are primarily related to individuals.

Leonard Oliver's book, *Study Circles: Coming Together for Personal Growth and Social Change*, provides an overview of the philosophical background to this type of model. Materials may be obtained from the Swedish

National Board of Education through their representatives for further information.

Notes

1. N.D. Kurland, "The Scandinavian Study Circle: An Idea for the U.S.," *Lifelong Learning: The Adult Years* V (February, 1982), p. 24.

2. D.W. Stewart, *Adult Learning in America: Eduard Lindeman and His Agenda for Lifelong Education* (Malabar, Fla.: Kreiger, 1987), p. 115.

3. An excellent description of the Swedish Folk School system may be found in the booklet, *The Swedish Folk High School*, published by the Swedish National Board of Education, Stockholm, in 1986. It is part of a series and was produced by the Information Section, Adult Education Department, Swedish National Board of Education.

4. Clay Warren, "Andragogy and N.F.S. Grundtwig: A Critical Link," *Adult Education Quarterly* 39: 4 (Summer, 1989), pp. 211-223.

5. Ibid., p. 219.

6. Leonard P. Oliver, *Study Circles: Coming Together for Personal Growth and Social Change* (Washington, D.C.: Seven Locks Press, 1987).

7. Ibid., pp. 22-28.

8. Ibid., p. xvii, and *The Adult Education Associations in Sweden: Study Circles and Cultural Activities in the People's Own Educational Work* (Stockholm: The National Swedish Federation of Adult Education), pp. 3-4.

9. Ibid., p. 7.

Chapter 17

A "Pedagogy"
For Adult Religious Education

This model reflects the commitment to community learning which is inherent in the "pedagogy" of the radical adult educator, Paulo Freire. This is a model which involves people in changing their world, not just themselves. It involves the sharing of experience, the creation of new levels of understanding, and concerted action.

Paulo Freire created considerable discussion in the education community with his writings. *Pedagogy of the Oppressed*[1] and subsequent works such as *Education for Critical Consciousness*,[2] and *Cultural Action for Freedom*[3] have introduced us to an approach to education which comes from a Third World experience. I believe the third world does have much to share with us, and the examination of his approach could confirm that belief for you.

One strong indication of this success in Brazil may be found in the fact that a repressive government of that country found it necessary to pressure Paulo Freire into leaving after it became aware of his work in literacy with the poor. However, the only substantial evidence of its success is regrettably anecdotal.

The model will provide vehicles for community and social action. There will be moments in the context of the faith community, and the larger community in which the faith community functions, when social action is required. Each community will make such a decision on the basis of its nature and situation as to the need for its commitment to social action. When a choice is made to explore the need for social action, this model and the following model will provide options for consideration.

138

Many models and methods of education emphasize the individual nature of learning, and the group serves the purpose of supporting the person's individual learning. Such an approach will not be conducive to the community acting together as much as to individual action. When it is desired that the faith community should act, a process of learning and growth in concert will enable the community to act.

There are certain essential elements to remember when the implementation of this model is considered. The first element is the avoidance of the "banking" concept of education. The second element involves the process of "conscientization" which results in analysis and understanding. The third element is "praxis."

The banking concept is an oppressive view of education which sees the teacher as the source of all knowledge, skill, and so on, while the learner is merely the receptacle.[4] This places much pressure on the teacher who must demonstrate continuously the highest level of expertise. It also denies the experience, knowledge, and skills of the learner.

Freire proposes an alternative to the "contradictions" inherent in the banking model by suggesting reconciliation of the positions. He suggests that "both are simultaneously teachers and students."[5] The experience, knowledge, and skills of all parties to the learning activity are recognized.

What we have is the placement of teacher and learner on an equal basis of status which provides appropriate recognition. The key to the situation is mutual recognition and respect. The same equality of a society which eliminates oppression should be the hallmark of the classroom.

The second element is the element of understanding which Freire refers to as "conscientization."[6] This is clearly the type of understanding which emerges from knowledge and analysis. It involves the awareness which enables changes to occur in the context of a society.

This conscientization is realized through the process of dialogue. Freire refers to this form of dialogue as within the "horizontal relationship between persons."[7] The parties are engaged in a common search for truth, thus we can see the commitment to an interactive communication model.

"Praxis" is the term Freire uses to describe the interaction between action and reflection or theory and practice.[8] This word has an important connotation for me. It involves the improvement of practice through its careful examination in the light of theoretical consideration over time.

The nature of the process can be seen in the examination of experience which provides the base for a theoretical understanding of the situation. One then proceeds to act under the influence of the new theoretical understanding of the situation. This will be followed by a period in which experiences are reexamined with the intention to further develop one's theoretical understanding. The continuation of this process will result in "praxis."

We should describe "praxis" as the theoretically based action or practice of the thoughtful practitioner. What could be more appropriate for those who would achieve changes in lifestyle and community situations.

Both White[9] and Groome see the value of the concepts of conscientization and praxis in the religious education process. Groome describes the stages of this process in his book, *Christian Religious Education*.[10] This is clearly a way of changing behavior in the context of religion.

What I personally found to be most important in the approach of Freire in the classroom, during my brief experience in his "class," was his respect and warmth for those other persons who were sharing the experience. This truly religious person was committed to recognizing the value in all persons. If we want to develop a model which bears any true relationship to his name, we must attempt to include this important dimension of his approach to people.

Freire began his writing after his extensive work in the Third World context, but this writing does have much to teach others from outside the Third World. Injustice is not confined to other places, nor is the need for social action.

The major advantage of this model is that it enables people to act with conviction and knowledge based upon a creative learning process. The result of this process for participants is a higher degree of commitment to community action than one can achieve with the andragogical model or many other individual or group models.

The disadvantages inherent in the model come from the group commitment. An individual who wishes to pursue personal growth and change separate from others will not wish to engage in this interdependent model.

METHODOLOGY

The methodology of this approach must avoid the style prevalent in many classroom settings. An introductory experience of climate setting will be useful, but it should not attempt to "preach" a method to the participants. Explanations should occur in limited fashion and, if possible, in small groups. An understanding of the model should emerge over time and be seen to do so.

The life experience of the individual in the community and the characteristics of the community need to be shared by the members of the group. This involves telling the story. The analysis will evolve out of the story and the subsequent discussions of the story.

When Freire was concerned about the teaching of literacy, as is described in the book, *Education for Critical Consciousness*, a single word often provided the focus for dialogue.[11] This dialogue is the approach he clearly favors for an appropriate educational process.[12]

Because people must tell their own story, the learning process clearly begins with where they are. There is little opportunity for the teacher to impose a presupposition if the story begins with a description of the life situations of the group members. This will open the dialogue.

Once the dialogue has begun and people are involved, the next step is to find the key components to the stories. The processes of "thematic breakdown" and "codification" allow us to identify these key components and to understand them.

To define this situation in another way, we need to discover first what is important and then to understand why it is important. An analysis of society is vital to this process. Learners will discover information as part of the process of analysis.

The "leader" in this context will share some information with the other learners. He or she may assist the group to discover sources of information about issues. The other manner in which the "leader" can facilitate is through the process of questioning for clarification and demarcation of issues. Freire also used the opportunity toward the end of the session to share his observations and responses.

The standard approach in this process could involve the following steps:

1. The group is involved in introductory sharing of a brief nature in order to establish relations.
2. A "story" is shared by a member of the group (relevant life experience).
3. Other members share their responses.
4. Critical issues are identified.
5. Further information is gathered about the issues and shared (perhaps over several sessions).
6. The analysis of the situation continues and deepens over time.
7. Decisions for action are taken by the group.
8. Follow-up of actions occurs through shared group sessions.

The amount of time required for analysis will vary depending upon the situation which the group is attempting to examine.

There is an intention that the process be used to develop a close sense of relationship among the learners. The word "solidarity" conveys the sense of commitment to a common cause and social action. The ability to work effectively together may be a desired outcome which will result from this process.

Another factor which may be important to learners in the context of this model is the learner's sense of confidence and self-worth. It is the responsibility of the teacher (or facilitator) to assist the student to learn successfully, thereby contributing to a positive sense of self as an individual and as a member of the group.

Although this model strongly reflects its Third World roots, I think that we should consider the possibility that many learners in our faith communities will lack a positive image of themselves and others around them. The activity of learning successfully together in order to achieve common goals will help us change this limited view of self and others.

People should be encouraged to express their views and the experiences which assist in the formation of these views. They should be encouraged to obtain new information for the group also. This process should involve sharing and not domination by any party. A sense of trust is important in order to prevent people from feeling that anything shared will be used against them.

As the group begins to accumulate information, the process of analysis through the use of the "theme" should begin. This involves a recognition of the factors which come together in our society to cause the situation to be as it is. Freire sees individuals as contributors to the culture in which they live.[13]

By isolating and examining specific situations, we can examine the factors contributing to these situations in our society. The key is to identify and break down the situation for accurate and appropriate analysis.

The level of understanding will increase to the point where the ability to intervene becomes a factor. As the individual and group develop the ability to understand and to intervene they will begin to make choices as to how to use these new skills. The choices must be made by the people themselves!

The role of the teacher or facilitator in this model is not to decide how the group will act or what they will do to intervene in society. The choice of action is to be left to the group. The facilitator should participate and enable without directing.

Figure 1:

A Pedagogy of Adult Religious Education

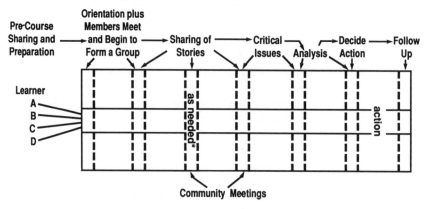

* "As needed" refers to the holding of meetings as required.

A key issue in this model will be making the choice of an appropriate response to the learning which has occurred. It is critical that the process be democratic and appropriate. Learners will decide jointly where to proceed.

The proposed process for this decision making should involve a series of steps to precede the final decision. I suggest the following guidelines:

1. A review of the relevant facts to be used in the process.
2. A list of the suggestions of possible actions to be collected from all participants.
3. Careful examination of each alternative in turn to insure that the possibilities are understood.
4. A democratic process of decision making which results in a decision. The most preferred mode would involve a consensus within the group which will result in commitment to the decision.

The last point may require some further comment. Certainly there are other democratic decision-making possibilities which might be used. A consensus decision-making process will enable all parties to reach the decision to have a sense of involvement in the results. This will be consistent with the process of the group at other stages where their ideas and experiences were valued fully.

The critical issue of commitment has already been noted. If we wish to have commitment and involvement in the activity which is to follow a decision for action, we must decide to do everything possible to insure that this occurs. It would be a shame to lose the momentum and commitment created in the earlier process to a process which does not have involvement.

SUMMARY COMMENTS

It appears that there are tremendous advantages in the use of this type of model with people who are disadvantaged and who have low levels of literacy. The Third World has seen the basic model used to considerable effect, and some disadvantaged community groups have found it most useful in the North American context.

The advantages of this model include the community commitment which emerges through implementation and capacity to involve learners in meaningful ways. This model has reached those who have been unsuccessful learners in other models.

A disadvantage of this model is its inability to work in individualized ways with learners over the long term. Each person will receive some opportunity for input, but numbers preclude sufficient time for longer periods of study on a topic which is not of some importance to the group.

The effectiveness of this model in relation to literacy issues has been proven by the rise to prominence of the educator who developed it. People in Brazil and elsewhere did learn to read and to transform their communities in a manner derived from the basic model of Freire.

Those who wish to learn more about this model should read *Pedagogy of the Oppressed* and *Education for Critical Consciousness*.

Notes

1. Paulo Freire, *Pedagogy of the Oppressed* (New York: Seabury, 1970).
2. Paulo Freire, *Education for Critical Consciousness* (New York: Seabury, 1973).
3. Paulo Freire, *Cultural Action for Freedom* (Cambridge, Mass.: Harvard Educational Review and Center for the Study of Development and Social Change, 1970).
4. Freire, *Pedagogy of the Oppressed*, pp. 58-59.
5. Ibid., p. 59.
6. Ibid., pp. 19-21.
7. Freire, *Education for Critical Consciousness*, p. 45.
8. Ibid., p. 75.
9. James W. White, *Intergenerational Religious Education: Models, Theory, and Prescription for Interage Life and Learning in the Faith Community* (Birmingham, Ala.: Religious Education Press, 1988), pp. 138-140.
10. Thomas H. Groome, *Christian Religious Education: Sharing our Story and Vision* (San Francisco: Harper & Row, 1980), pp. 207-208.
11. Freire, *Education for Critical Consciousness*, pp. 82-84.
12. Ibid., p. 45.
13. Ibid., p. 47.

Chapter 18

The Action Research Model

This is a model which enables group self-directed learning
through a combination of the ideas taken from new activities in
the area of Action Research and the emerging area of Participatory
Research. It has the ability to support efforts to define, analyze,
and provide solutions for community problems through the creation of new knowledge, understanding, and action.

This model is derived from activities which have been known by such
names as "participatory" or "action" research, but the essential idea is the gathering of information and the participation of concerned parties in a process
which leads to social change. Beverly Cassara has described it in the following
manner:

Participatory Research is an important adult education idea — a powerful
democratic idea that enables social groups, deprived of education and eco-
nomic and political advantages, to gain some mastery over their own development.[1]

She also states that this model differs from the traditional approach to
self-directed learning which is individual in nature. The category in which this
falls is "group self-directed learning."[2]

Some people may regard this model's origins as solely research oriented,
which it can be if taken from one perspective. If the model is seen from the
eyes of the "academic" or the "professional" researcher, it may be viewed as
a research model. The alternative perspective is from the eyes of the persons
from the community who engage in the process with the researcher. Then it
may be seen as a model for the support of learning. This chapter will attempt

to enlarge on that latter perspective and the ways in which the researcher can support the process.

It is my contention that while the research process may be important to a particular aspect of this model, the learning process for most participants is the most valuable component. The participants become learners in a process which provides for exemplary group involvement and action.

Research may be described as either the creation or the discovery of "new" knowledge. Insofar as this model breaks away from the traditional form of "knowledge" found in papers, books, journals, and so on, it ceases to be a "commodity" of traditional research institutions.[3] This model represents a unique achievement in the creative process. The learners or participants in the process achieve a new and dynamic understanding of knowledge as they all contribute to their own understanding (and the researcher's) of a social context through the creation of "new" knowledge.

This approach to research has been seen in what has been called "participatory" research. I was tempted to use that title for this proposed model, but I prefer to use the word *action* in the title for its positive connotations. The comparability of the two approaches is demonstrated quite well by the inclusion of a chapter on "action research" by Michael Pilsworth and Ralph Ruddock in a major text on participatory research entitled *Creating Knowledge: A Monopoly*, edited by Budd Hall et al.[4]

Participation is a key element in both research models. The community group becomes a part of the process of the research through "participation" which is one goal of the process. I prefer to emphasize the "action" component because I believe that it is not sufficient for the community simply to come together. The community must come together in order to do something. Participation will make it possible, but action must happen for the "coming together" to become most meaningful.

There should be no doubt in anyone's mind that the purpose of this model is group action which leads to social change. If this particular goal is not considered to be appropriate for your faith community, this model should not be utilized.

If the goal of community involvement and social change is an appropriate one for your faith community, do not hesitate to consider and use this model. This type of approach has proven to be effective in other settings and in limited use in certain faith communities. A commitment to its basic premises is essential.

The theoretical base for this model owes much to the work of Budd Hall and his colleagues in the Participatory Research Group of the International Council for Adult Education and the writings of Chris Argyris and his colleagues. The book entitled *Action Science* by Argyris, Putnam, and Smith[5] provides certain key theoretical considerations which influenced the development of this model for social change.

Hall, in a separate article, lists certain basic concepts of participatory research. The following points should be considered in relation to this model:

1. The problem originates in the community itself and the problem is defined, analyzed, and solved by the community.
2. The ultimate goal of research is the radical transformation of social reality and the improvement of the lives of the people involved.
3. Participatory Research involves the full and active participation of the community in the center of the research process.
4. The process of participatory research can create a greater awareness in the people of their own resources and mobilize them for self-reliant development.[6]

In reference to *Action Science* by Argyris, Putnam, and Smith, the combination of the two key components of the book's title, action and science, is essential. I like to think of it as combining "inquiry" with "relevant activity" on the part of the learners. A full chapter of the book is devoted to the consideration of "promoting learning through action and change.[7] This is a critical aspect of this model for me. Learning occurs in the context of the desire for action and change and is shaped by the process.

The definition of content or knowledge to be learned is critical to this model. I offer the following points drawn, in part, from Argyris, Putnam, and Smith as indicative of the considerations which will make this model work.

1. Knowledge should consider human limitations and be oriented to action.
2. Knowledge should assist in the formation of a sense of direction without assuming prior statements of goals and objectives as given.
3. Knowledge should take into account the values and norms of people in order to be meaningful.[8]

We are searching in fact for knowledge which is creative, useful, and meaningful to ourselves and our group.

There are three other dimensions of the process of learning which find worthwhile comments in these authors' work. They include the following points:

1. Helping the learners to be reflective and to experiment with ideas and their applications.
2. Expanding the learning in all directions in order to see all possibilities.
3. Developing new terms of reference to assist in action.

These three points allow us to see how to create the learning process within the model.

METHODOLOGY

I propose a specific approach to this model which incorporates ideas for learning and research. The stages are rather different for this model and should be considered carefully before proceeding.

1. Discuss the situation with key people in the community, preferably in some form of small group setting, in order to obtain community-based support for the activity. Please note that nothing will happen without this support.
2. Plan a meeting which will enable people to come together to express their concerns about the community. They may express their hopes as well.
3. Use the traditional methods and any other effective methods of communication within the community which reach all parts of the community, particularly those persons who are hard to reach. Indicate the commitment to respond to community concerns.
4. Use the initial meeting to orient people to the general approach, but do not prolong the discussion as the model will unfold. The orientation to deal with community concerns is the key issue.
5. Begin the process of gathering data to be used by the group. This may include sources identified by the group members as well as by the facilitator. This is an ongoing process.
6. Add new data to the pool of knowledge and open the process to further exploration of the old and new issues raised and their implications.
7. Assist the processing of new data to shape the sense of future directions and actions of the group.
8. Assist the group to begin to determine actions to be taken.
9. Assistance in the implementation of actions and further data collection should continue simultaneously.
10. Support the expansion of ideas and review of activities to date.
11. Enable the review of data and results of action to be ongoing and the continuous search for data until the desired results have been achieved.

See Figure 1 for an overview of the process.

Figure 1:

Action – Research

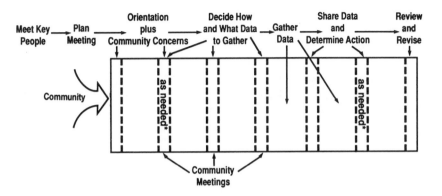

* "As needed" refers to the holding of meetings as required.

True change in society has its roots in work with people. The need to be trusted by people is critical to this process. Individuals who are not part of the group within a community who are trusted and regarded as leaders must obtain the visible support and commitment of those who have this status. The purpose of step number 1 is primarily to obtain this essential indicator.

For many leaders in the faith community this step may appear to be satisfied already. Be certain that the expectations people have of you do not preclude the possibility of your engaging in this form of learning process for change.

A further reason for step number 1 is the need to have people provide leadership in the learning process. The facilitator can receive much needed assistance to maintain and to sustain the learning process.

People are prepared to share their hopes, dreams, and concerns in an atmosphere of trust within their own community group. This will only happen if you prepare a meeting which incorporates all members of the community and makes them feel comfortable.

It is particularly important to communicate that all members of the community who wish to be involved will be included in the process. There should be a serious attempt made to insure that all parties feel welcome and involved from the very beginning.

If a part of your group does not respond to a particular form of advertising, do not be afraid to use more than one format for information sharing. Word of mouth should be encouraged as one very effective way to get community commitment and involvement. People will be encouraged to come if there is a real concern in the community, and there is some hope that it will be the focus of activity for improvement.

Good climate setting activities should be used from the beginning but remember that these people have existing relationships. A comfortable arrangement of seats and tables plus easy activities will enable the appropriate climate to develop.

Remember that people are more interested in results than the fancy explanation of a "model." They will need to know enough to convince them to proceed but no more is required. Use the first session to get commitment to discuss the issues which will lead into the process of learning. If they feel that they are discussing relevant issues, they are likely to return.

As the issues, concerns, and so on, unfold, the group will begin to realize that it needs more information in order to understand fully and to achieve results through effective action. Assist group members to identify, locate, and gather information which can then be shared with the others. Avoid the temptation to be the sole source as to the location of information or the sole person to provide it to the group. This process is about their learning. The ability to gather information is as important in the long term as the ownership of knowledge is in the short term.

As information is gathered and assessed, the group should use it to influence the sense of direction and actions which will be taken to achieve the desired goals. Action should be encouraged as the group becomes ready to act. It is through action that confidence will grow and the opportunity to assess the impact of the learning will occur.

The process must continue as new data becomes available based upon results from action as well as other data collection. The evaluation of action is critical to maintain the group's sense of commitment to change. The group must be prepared to undertake this in an honest and open manner at this stage of the process.

There is no real end to this kind of process in a faith community. Once people have begun to understand the power derived from communal activity, it will be difficult to persuade them to cease to use it. The nature of the group may shift as will the sense of direction, priorities, and so on. The key will be the ability to maintain a sense of direction which is related to the needs of the community.

The researcher will prepare his report on the research component of the process at this stage. I suggest that this be done in concert with the participants and that the results in print or other form be shared with the community. In one instance, a community with which I had worked chose to write and perform a play to demonstrate the nature of their "learning."

SUMMARY COMMENTS

This is a creative, self-sustaining model for adult learning which is focused upon the community rather than the individual learner. Its true value will be found in the way in which it is used to transform the faith community. No community can expect to be unchanged as a result of a learning process, but this model will guarantee significant change. I hasten to add that it must be done appropriately in order to achieve these results.

The negative aspect of this model is that changes are not desired by all. Should there be a large group opposed to change, it will be more difficult to achieve the desired results. Splits have been known to occur in communities where this model is used. Caution is advised to all who would use this model.

Another serious issue is that the model can be subverted by the few who wish to manipulate the community for their own ends. It is important to insure that the community defines the problem and acts to solve it.

The model will insure maximum participation and effective action when used appropriately. The research of numerous groups has proven effective and provocative.

Notes

1. Beverly B. Cassara, *Participatory Research: Group Self-Directed Learning for Social Transformation* (Athens, Ga.: Adult Education Department, College of Education, University of Georgia, 1987), p. 1.

2. Ibid., p. 2.

3. Budd Hall, "Knowledge as Commodity and Participatory Research" *Prospects* I.IX: 4 (1979).

4. Michael Pilsworth and Ralph Ruddock, "Persons, Not Respondents: Alternative Approaches in the Study of Social Process," in *Creating Knowledge: A Monopoly*, ed. Budd Hall, Arthur Gillette, and Rajesh Tandon (New Delhi, India: Society for Participatory Research in Asia, 1982). See the explanation of action theory on page 69.

5. Chris Argyris, Robert Putnam, and Diana McLain Smith, *Action Science* (San Francisco: Jossey-Bass, 1987).

6. Hall, "Knowledge as a Commodity and Participatory Research," pp. 19-20.

7. Argyris, Putnam, and McLain Smith, *Action Science*, chapter 2.

8. Ibid., pp. 36 and 37.

Chapter 19

Distance Education

> Distance education is characterized by Desmond Keegan as having the following components: some separation of teacher and learner throughout the process, an organization which plans and prepares the materials, use of technical media (print, audio, video, computer) to unite teacher and learner, a two-way communication process, and the "quasi-permanent absence of the learning group."[1]

Distance education is a growing phenomenon on a worldwide basis. It is being used in many formats by many agencies in order to reach a wider group of clients than the traditional approaches can reach. As Keegan suggests, it is characterized by some degree of separation from the teacher and the other learners as well as varied methods and an organization to prepare and deliver materials.

Churches have recognized for a considerable time the value of providing opportunities for growth and learning at a distance, just as secular institutions have done. We should recognize, nevertheless, that the level of required sophistication in one's approach to distance education has increased considerably over the years for both secular and religious agencies.

There is a long tradition of public and private correspondence agencies of various types in the United States and elsewhere in the world.[2] More recently, secular agencies throughout North America, Europe, and elsewhere have utilized the various media including such vehicles as television, radio, computers, satellites, fiber optics, and numerous others to move beyond the traditional print method of distance delivery.[3]

This chapter will not review the history of developments in distance education nor will it provide a comprehensive overview of all present-day activities. It will be limited to a description of the guidelines which will enable effective delivery and insure that this sometimes expensive model is applied more appropriately in the religious setting. More extensive reviews are provided elsewhere in the literature on the development of distance education.

There are many adults for whom the normal schedule of life precludes participation in either full-time or part-time studies through the standard course or classroom format. The inability to be available for all meetings of a course will cause difficulties for shift workers or persons with demanding commitments. There are also many people who are unable, because of disability or a similar problem, to leave one location to travel to another. It is important to remember that adults do not learn only from 7:00 to 9:30 on Tuesday evenings for six weeks.

Michael Moore argues quite strongly in an article on distance education for the responsible role of the learner in the process.[4] I believe that this includes the important issue of self-pacing along with other aspects of decision making. This model will enable us to serve the autonomous and busy adult who can not take advantage of other program opportunities or for whom such opportunities do not exist.

Distance education helps us to reach the relatively inaccessible adult in the settings where they wish to do their learning. No adult needs to feel that his or her needs are not being considered when the distance option is made available for those who cannot or do not wish to choose the more standard course formats.

Many distance education institutions from around the world provide us with a wealth of experience to draw upon in order to establish effective approaches to this area of program activity. I have visited several of these institutions in order to gather detailed knowledge of their operations.[5]

Borje Holmberg has provided a set of guidelines for course development which are drawn from his experience and observations of many distance education programs. It is his view that the didactic approach should exhibit these characteristics:

1. Clear, readable, uncrowded presentation of materials.
2. Specific suggestions for the learning process, including things to avoid.
3. An invitation to question, to accept or reject on solid grounds after careful consideration.
4. Attempts to involve the student on a personal level in the subject.
5. Personal writing style.
6. Clearly demarcated changes in theme through use of print, voice, or other appropriate means.[6]

The important components should include course development, but we must look beyond that in order to maximize our options for success. Moore also notes the importance of the role of the educator in support of the learning process in his article on self-directed learning and distance education.[7] The system we organize to support the adult's learning must prevent misunderstanding, difficulties, and drop-outs from our programs. It is the support system which will make our distance education model work, once we have the courses and programs planned, developed, and available.

This chapter will include comments on both the course "production" process and the implementation phase which involves working with the learners. We need to remember that the best planned courses can have problems if they are not organized appropriately to make them work properly.

METHODOLOGY

It is necessary to begin with a planning and development process to begin the creation of the distance education option. No system for implementation can save a course or program which is not well-planned and developed from the outset. The implementation of program will be discussed more fully in the following section.

Program Planning

The Open University in Britain and other similar institutions have shown that the quality of people involved in the process is critical. The use of outside academics of considerable experience combined with technical experts and internal academic specialists enabled the Open University to provide top-quality courses.[8]

The following proposals can provide a higher likelihood of success for any distance education program. They are suggestions which are derived largely from observations of the Open University as well as from the literature.

1. A skilled team of course developers should be involved in the preparation of any program for distance delivery. The team's requirements will be determined by the technical expertise needed for delivery and the content expertise needed to cover the topic(s) involved.
2. A network of people should be involved in program delivery. This network should include specialists at the central core and local contact persons who can assist the learner directly.
3. Virtually all members of the team should have training both before delivery and after the system has been put into operation to insure the needed skills for this special mode of delivery.
4. Learners should be able to identify a person who is available in person or by telephone for the direct communication of concerns, questions, and so on.
5. In-person meetings may be arranged where feasible and are particularly helpful with persons new to this mode of delivery.

6. Programs should be reviewed and revised on a regular and appropriate basis.
7. Material should be in modular format, wherever possible, in order to insure maximum flexibility for maximum use by a broad range of learners.
8. Cooperation between institutions will insure the maximum commitment of resources to provide the best possible quality and distribution of programs.

Perhaps some comment on each of these items will assist the reader to see the key aspects of each suggestion.

The preparation of good course materials requires more than a knowledgeable subject matter specialist. Good writing skills and publishing skills are required to insure readable printed products. Distance packages will often contain visual and audio materials, thus necessitating technical expertise in the media to be utilized.

Doing the work without experts will result in packages which are less attractive and useful to the learner. I was struck recently by a well-written package which had so little "white space" that it would intimidate most learners immediately by its volume. A team approach should be taken with respect for each member and his or her expertise. The team can work together to provide the requisite components of the package.

One rule, which has often been stated by my Open University colleagues, is to allow for the primacy of the content specialist in the team. Nothing should be done which violates content integrity.[9]

The Open University's success is strongly related to its capacity to provide a support network for learners. This includes a strong central core of specialists with liaison responsibility and a team of local contact persons who provide support to local learners.

When I think of the institutional churches, synagogues, and so on, which exist on a wide basis to support our people in worship and other things, I see the potential for a national system of distance education on an ecumenical or individual institutional basis. We also have many specialists from the secular world within our faith communities. The expertise is potentially available. We need only to harness and to train the people in the system.

I have already alluded to the need for training of staff in the distance mode of delivery. Most educators are more familiar with the face-to-face models of education. The system will work far better if these people are helped to work in a different way within this alternative model. My conversations with the Open University staff have convinced me of the value they perceive in training events for themselves and the part-time staff in the regional locations.

The methods I propose be used for the training of staff will include both training materials and in-person meetings (where possible). The distance mode may present problems to the new staff person with experience exclusively in face-to-face delivery. A general orientation can help to create a useful link between the local contact person and those responsible in a central location for course coordination.

The knowledge and skill required for staff will provide a focus for the training. Complete familiarity with the learning materials should be combined with skills for working with people either through telephone contact or short-term personal interaction with individuals or tutorial groups.

The Open University uses a system which involves the forwarding of mailings from a central location while local contact persons are available to work directly with the students. The best training program I have observed in this institution includes the examination on a regular basis of the very real problems which staff face in interactions with learners.

We can assume that many learners will have problems, questions, or issues which they need to discuss on an immediate basis on occasion. Both telephone links and in-person communication can help to avoid frustrations and to help the learner gain the most from the learning process. Knowing that it is a simple matter of making a quick telephone call in order to get support can help the student to persevere if all is not going well.

If learners are not too isolated, it may be feasible to initiate some in-person meetings between individual learners or groups and the institution's local expert. These meetings have been found to be of considerable value to learners and staff alike.

The pattern of bringing people together for short residential experiences should be considered as a valuable option. The isolation is less when there is a sense of the commitment of other known persons. Telephone contact takes on a more human dimension when prior personal meetings have occurred.

There is also a possibility that the learning does need some interaction for part of the process. Under these circumstances, the meeting can be used for interaction while preparation is done at a distance in advance.

No material should be permitted to last forever without a review to insure its continued relevance! I believe that both content experts and students should be consulted in the review process. Revisions should occur as needed using the team approach in order to provide continued quality.

It is possible to find additional uses for material which is not limited by a tight, narrow format. If it is necessary to follow the entire course for some particular reason, then do prepare this type of course. If it is possible to be flexible, and I believe that this is quite often the case, be flexible!

A flexible format will enable local resource persons or other contact persons to provide the parts of the package relevant to those for whom the whole package is not. The decision to use part of the package can be made by the learner and his or her contact person.

The ability of one institution to provide high quality material across a wide range of content areas is limited in most religious institutions in North America and elsewhere. It is likely that the best results will be achieved by cooperation between religious groups and other agencies with educational commitments. The Open University's cooperation with the British Broadcasting Corporation is a good example of what can be achieved when both parties can satisfy their interests.

This is a methodological concern because the methods available to the programers will be limited by lack of expertise and other resources. Perhaps ecumenical cooperation is not too much to ask for in the 1990s.

Implementation

Many of the points suggested for planning will be followed in the implementation phase. The following points summarize key issues from the prior list and add some new ideas to be considered:

1. All facilitators and teachers should be well-trained in order to maximize the effectiveness of the implementation phase.
2. Learners should be provided with an orientation to this approach to learning.
3. Learners should be provided with an accessible and approachable contact person who will guide and support them while in the system.
4. In-person sessions should occur at early stages to give people the confidence and support needed to proceed.
5. Materials on content and for support activities should be provided on a regular basis with the intention of keeping the student active but not overloaded.
6. The learner should be assisted to withdraw from the process at the end of the learning or at any other time, if necessary.

Any implementation of an idea will depend upon the quality of the people involved and their understanding of their role in the implementation process. Training in distance education and the specific responsibilities of a particular program or course will give the local facilitator confidence and skills to perform the required tasks.

Many learners have insufficient experience with distance education to enter a program without an orientation. Both materials and personal orientation can assist the learner to become more aware of the future requirements of the new situation.

A personal contact can be critical to a learner's feeling of comfort and confidence. A meeting with the facilitator or teacher can enable growth of a personal relationship which supports the learner through the difficult times and maximizes learning at other times.

Many distance education institutions have developed packages of materials which they provide to learners during orientation and at other appropriate times in the process. The Athabasca University of Alberta, Canada, has provided its students with excellent packages to support orientation of the learner to the new institution.[10]

The Open University also encourages its Centers to send materials to students who have dropped out in order to inform them of their rights to return and to offer assistance to obtain counseling if the situation requires it. The withdrawal from learning, either through successful completion or other reasons, can be a difficult experience. If there are examinations to be passed, the experience for adults can be traumatic. Special materials to assist for withdrawal or examination preparation should be provided to students at the appropriate time.

SUMMARY COMMENTS

Distance Education can enable us to reach a wide range of people who are inaccessible through other models for course delivery. Materials can be adapted to a wide range of needs and interests while making use of any appropriate technology. The benefits can spread well beyond the community which we normally serve. Learners who are new to us can make use of our otherwise inaccessible institutional resources.

There are disadvantages to distance education which must be considered prior to a decision to proceed. The following factors should be considered a serious deterrent to any distance education initiative:

1. The content of the course requires considerable human interaction in order to be taught properly.
2. The learners require a considerable amount of support and involvement on an ongoing basis from the resource persons rather than from the material resources of a course.
3. Some form of local support system or some form of alternative communication link is not available to support the process of learning.
4. The learning process for distance learners can be highly individualistic. Many individual learners dislike learning in isolation from other persons when this is an extensive part of the learning process.

These conditions suggest that an alternative model is more likely to achieve the requisite successful process of learning.

It is important to remember that this model will provide a definite increase in accessibility to your programs which no other model can provide. For further information concerning distance education, I suggest that the reader consult the second edition of Desmond Keegan's book, *Foundations of Distance Education.*

Notes

1. Desmond Keegan, *Foundations of Distance Education*, 2nd ed. (London: Routledge, 1990), p. 44.

2. Ibid., p. 126.

3. Ibid., pp. 84-100.

4. Michael Moore, "Self-Directed Learning and Distance Education," *Journal of Distance Education* 1: 1 (Fall, 1986), pp. 7-22.

5. Formal fact-finding visits have been arranged to such institutions as The Open University in the United Kingdom, The Open Learning Authority in British Columbia, and Athabasca University in Alberta. The Open Learning Authority provides a variety of distance education programs in many areas via several media.

6. Borje Holmberg, "Guided Didactic Conversation in Distance Education," in *Distance Education: International Perspectives*, ed. David Sewart, Desmond Keegan, and Borje Holmberg (London: Routledge, 1983), pp. 114-122.

7. Moore, "Self-Directed Learning and Distance Education," pp. 10-12.

8. Walter Perry, *The Open University: A Personal Account by the First Vice-Chancellor* (Milton Keynes, United Kingdom: Open University Press, 1976).

9. This point was stressed to me during my first period as a visiting professor at the Open University in Britain in 1985.

10. I recommend the *Athabasca University Student Handbook*, edited by Maxim Jean-Louis, and *Improve Your Study Skills: A Series of Seven Modules for Adult Students*, written by Virginia Nilsson. These materials were published by Athabasca University in 1985 and 1988 respectively.

Chapter 20

Concluding Remarks

The reader who has reached this stage in the book will probably have read a significant part of the preceding portion thereof. Perhaps what has been written here and in the cited works of other educators will have helped convince you of the benefits of the options presented. Your reading will have made you aware of the options which do exist. I hope that some of you will choose to utilize certain alternative models which feel comfortable and offer some promise of success with adults in your context.

The need for alternative models is demonstrated quite clearly by the lack of participation on the part of some members of our faith communities in the existing, traditional activities. This is not meant to suggest that we should neglect those who do utilize the existing opportunities for programed learning in the future. Instead we must strive to assist the other persons who do not attend to find more suitable opportunities for learning.

Our fate, should we choose to ignore other learners and their requirements, will be to suffer a similar response from them. They will ignore us! Should we prove to be useless to them in their growth and development, they will seek alternative means or even alternative communities within which to grow.

A varied group of learners will continue to be motivated by diverse ideas, concerns, needs, and interests. They will learn because they want to do so for a wide range of reasons. Their place in the faith community and the world beyond will be enhanced by the things they do learn and the successful ways those things once learned are applied.

Learners will be at work in the learning process whether we choose to be beside them or not. They will learn from all elements of creation in a manner which will exceed the human limitations of the situation.

Creation will contribute to the experience of learners even when we do not participate as educators in the process. It will occur to the learner outside of our classrooms that there is something most important in their environment. When such events occur, our response is critical to our future inclusion in their plans.

Our choice of alternative models will depend on several factors including the learner or learners, the content, the context, and ourselves. We must consider these factors and then make the choice with optimism and "faith."

Our faith communities will determine to some extent the nature of what is possible. The collective community will have some view to express as will individual learners. There may be moments of conflict between these positions. You should exercise reasonable caution under those circumstances.

The precise construction of our faith communities is so varied that it becomes difficult to comment upon their nature accurately. There are some things we might say without contradiction in too many situations. Please forgive me if you do not believe that the comment is fair to your faith community.

The most striking thing for me about the learning process and its relationship to faith is the diversity of things which will occur among the group of interested learners. Our knowledge and experience of religious communities makes us aware of the variety of people and the variety of wants, interests, and needs represented there. Our ability to recognize and respond to this variety is the issue.

Another thing I consider to be of great importance is the ability of people within the faith community to support each other in their respective journeys. Learners are most capable of recognizing each other as the process of learning excites and enervates or, on some occasions, challenges and frustrates. It is often difficult to hide enthusiasm or frustration!

There will be times when the journey causes us to see the inadequacies which exist beyond ourselves. These inadequacies may be in our faith community or in the community beyond this small portion, even to the farthest corners of the earth. When this recognition occurs, it may be necessary for us to work together to respond to the demands which the recognition of inadequacy imposes on us. After all, we often try to change when we find ourselves lacking. Why should we not try to change more than ourselves in a positive and constructive manner?

Our situation as religious educators requires that we be sensitive to the feelings within the community and that we respond accordingly to positive reactions of learners to each other. We must put them in touch with each other and enable their support as it also facilitates the learning process.

The models described in this book represent those which I believe will be most useful to the adult religious educator in the faith communities of our society. I have attempted to present certain models with which I have some experience. The result of this background is that I can comment with some confidence on the workability of the models.

Several of these models have been used extensively by me as well as other practitioners. The other models with which I have less experience have proven their value to colleagues over time. I do not feel that there is a single model in the book which is likely to fail, provided the advice for its selection and implementation is followed.

Any sensible practitioner or theoretician-practitioner will want to use models which promise to be reasonably successful. No one can guarantee success, but there is something to be said about models and methods which have worked on other occasions at other times. Read the comments and follow the suggestions in order to avoid failure.

Bibliography

Jerold W. Apps, *How to Improve Adult Education in Your Church* (Minneapolis: Augsburg, 1972).

Jerold W. Apps, *Improving Practice in Continuing Education* (San Francisco: Jossey-Bass, 1985).

Chris Argyris, Robert Putnam, and Diana McLain Smith, *Action Science* (San Francisco: Jossey-Bass, 1987).

Douglas R. Berdie and John F. Anderson, *Questionnaires: Their Design and Use* (Methuchen, N.J.: Scarecrow, 1974).

Benjamin S. Bloom, ed., *The Taxonomy of Educational Objectives: The Classification of Educational Goals; Handbook 1, Cognitive Domain* (New York: David McKay, 1969).

Benjamin S. Bloom, J. Thomas Hastings, and George F. Madaus, *Handbook on Formative and Summative Evaluation of Student Learning* (New York: McGraw-Hill, 1971).

Edgar J. Boone, *Developing Programs in Adult Education* (Englewood Cliffs, N.J.: Prentice-Hall, 1985).

David Boud, "A Facilitator's View of Adult Learning," in *Appreciating Adults Learning: From the Learners' Perspective*, ed. David Boud and Virginia Griffin (London: Kogan Page, 1987).

Stephen D. Brookfield, *Understanding and Facilitating Adult Learning* (San Francisco: Jossey-Bass, 1986).

Don S. Browning, *Generative Man: Psychoanalytical Perspectives* (Philadelphia: Westminster, 1972).

Beverly B. Cassara, *Participatory Research: Group Self-Directed Learning for Social Transformation* (Athens, Ga.: Adult Education Department, University of Georgia, 1987).

163

K. Patricia Cross, *Adults as Learners* (San Francisco: Jossey-Bass, 1986).

M.S. Devereux, *One in Every Five: A Survey of Adult Education in Canada* (Ottawa: Statistics Canada and Education Support Sector, Department of Secretary of State, 1985).

Hedley G. Dimock, *Groups: Leadership and Group Development*, rev. ed. (San Diego: University Associates, 1987).

Gregory Dunwoody, "A Descriptive Survey of Important Religious Learning Projects of Roman Catholic Adults in Early and Middle Adulthood" (Unpublished manuscript, circa 1987).

John L. Elias, *The Foundations and Practice of Adult Religious Education* (Malabar, Fla.: Kreiger, 1982).

Erik H. Erikson, *Childhood and Society*, 2nd ed. (New York: Norton, 1963).

Nancy T. Foltz, "Basic Principles of Adult Religious Education," in *Handbook of Adult Religious Education*, ed. Nancy T. Foltz (Birmingham, Ala.: Religious Education Press, 1986).

Nancy T. Foltz, ed., *Handbook of Adult Religious Education* (Birmingham, Ala.: Religious Education Press, 1986).

James W. Fowler, *Stages of Faith: The Psychology of Human Development and the Quest for Meaning* (San Francisco: Harper & Row, 1981).

James W. Fowler, "Faith and the Structuring of Meaning," in *Faith Development and Fowler*, ed. Craig Dykstra and Sharon Parks (Birmingham, Ala.: Religious Education Press, 1986).

Paulo Freire, *Cultural Action for Freedom* (Cambridge, Mass.: Harvard Educational Review and the Center for the Study of Development and Social Change, 1970).

Paulo Freire, *Pedagogy of the Oppressed* (New York: Seabury, 1970).

Paulo Freire, *Education for Critical Consciousness* (New York: Seabury, 1973).

Quentin H. Gessner, "Planning Conferences, Seminars, and Workshops," in *Priorities in Adult Education*, ed. David B. Rauch (New York: Macmillan, 1972).

V. Bailley Gillespie, *The Experience of Faith* (Birmingham, Ala.: Religious Education Press, 1988).

Roger L. Gould, *Transformation: Growth and Change in Adult Life* (New York: Simon and Schuster, 1978).

C. Hartley Gratton, *In Quest of Knowledge: A Historical Perspective on Adult Education* (New York: Association Press, 1955).

Gwynneth Griffith, "Images of Interdependence: Authority and Power in Teaching/Learning," in *Appreciating Adults Learning: From the Learners' Perspective*, ed. David Boud and Virginia Griffin (London: Kogan Page, 1987).

Thomas H. Groome, *Christian Religious Education: Sharing our Story and Vision* (San Francisco: Harper & Row, 1980).

Egon G. Guba and Yvonne S. Lincoln, *Effective Evaluation: Improving the Usefulness of Evaluative Results through Responsive and Naturalistic Approaches* (San Francisco: Jossey-Bass, 1987).

Lucy S. Guglielmino, "Development of the Self-Directed Learning Readiness Scale" (Ph.D. dissertation, University of Georgia, 1977).

Jurgen Habermas, *Knowledge and Human Interest* (Boston: Beacon, 1971).

Budd Hall, "Knowledge as Commodity and Participatory Research," *Prospects* 1: 9 (1979).

Robert J. Havighurst, *Developmental Tasks and Education* (New York: David McKay, 1961).

Borje Holmberg, "Guided Didactic Conversation in Distance Education," in *Distance Education: International Perspectives*, ed. D. Stewart, D. Keegan, and B. Holmberg (London: Routledge, 1983).

R.A. Horowitz, "Psychological Effects of the 'Open Classroom'," *Review of Educational Research* 49 (1979).

Cyril O. Houle, *The Inquiring Mind: A Study of the Adult Who Continues to Learn* (Madison: University of Wisconsin Press, 1961).

Cyril O. Houle, *The Design of Education* (San Francisco: Jossey-Bass, 1972).

Cyril O. Houle, *Patterns of Learning: New Perspectives on Life Span Education* (San Francisco: Jossey-Bass, 1984).

Cyril O. Houle, *Continuing Learning in the Professions* (San Francisco: Jossey-Bass, 1984).

John M. Hull, *What Prevents Christian Adults from Learning?* (London: SCM Press, 1985).

Maxim Jean-Louis, ed., *Athabasca University Student Handook* (Athabasca, Canada: Athabasca University Press, 1985).

David W. Johnston and Frank P. Johnston, *Joining Together: Group Theory and Group Skills*, 3rd ed. (Englewood Cliffs, N.J.: Prentice-Hall, 1987).

John W.C. Johnstone and Ramon J. Rivera, *Volunteers for Learning: A Study of the Educational Pursuits of American Adults* (Chicago: Aldine, 1965).

Bruce Joyce and Marsha Weil, *Models of Teaching*, 3rd ed. (Englewood Cliffs, N.J.: Prentice-Hall, 1986).

Desmond Keegan, *Foundations of Distance Education*. 2nd ed. (London: Routledge, 1990).

James R. Kidd, *How Adults Learn*, rev. ed. (New York: Cambridge Press, 1973).

Malcolm S. Knowles, *The Modern Practice of Adult Education: Pedagogy versus Andragogy* (Houston: Gulf Publishing, 1970).

Malcolm S. Knowles, *Self-Directed Learning: A Guide for Learners and Teachers* (Chicago: Follett, 1975).

Malcolm S. Knowles, *The Modern Practice of Adult Education: From Pedagogy to Andragogy*, revised and updated (Chicago: Follett, 1980).

Malcolm S. Knowles, *Using Learning Contracts: Practical Approaches to Individualizing and Structuring Learning* (San Francisco: Jossey-Bass, 1986).

David A. Kolb, *Experiential Learning: Experience as the Source of Learning and Development* (Englewood Cliffs, N.J.: Prentice-Hall, 1984).

N.D. Kurland, "The Scandinavian Study Circle: An Idea for the U.S.," *Lifelong Learning: The Adult Years* 5 (February, 1982).

Gordon Lawrence, *People Types and Tiger Stripes: A Practical Guide to Learning Styles*, 2nd ed. (Gainesville, Fla.: Center for Applications of Psychological Type, 1982).

James M. Lee, "The Authentic Source of Religious Instruction," in *Religious Education and Theology*, ed. Norma H. Thompson (Birmingham, Ala.: Religious Education Press, 1982).

James M. Lee, *The Content of Religious Instruction: A Social Science Approach* (Birmingham, Ala.: Religious Education Press, 1985)

Daniel J. Levinson et al., *The Seasons of a Man's Life* (New York: Ballantine Books, 1978).

James E. Loder, *The Transformational Moment: Understanding Convictional Experiences* (San Francisco: Harper & Row, 1981).

Carolyn M. Mamchur, *Insights: Understanding Yourself and Others* (Toronto: The Ontario Institute for Studies in Education, 1984).

Abraham H. Maslow, *Motivation and Personality* (New York: Harper and Brothers, 1970).

Leon McKenzie, *The Religious Education of Adults* (Birmingham, Ala.: Religious Education Press, 1982).

Leon McKenzie, "The Purposes and Scope of Adult Religious Education," in *Handbook of Adult Religious Education*, ed. Nancy T. Foltz (Birmingham, Ala.: Religious Education Press, 1986).

Sharon B. Merriam and Trenton R. Ferro, "Working with Young Adults," in *Handbook of Adult Religious Education*, ed. Nancy T. Foltz (Birmingham, Ala.: Religious Education Press, 1986).

Michael Moore, "Self-Directed Learning and Distance Education," *Journal of Distance Education* 1: 1 (Fall, 1986).

Virginia Nillson, *Improve Your Study Skills: A Series of Seven Modules for Adult Students* (Athabasca, Canada: Athabasca University, 1988).

Henri Nouwen, *Reaching Out: The Three Movements of the Spiritual Life* (Garden City, N.Y.: Doubleday, 1975).

Leonard P. Oliver, *Study Circles: Coming Together for Personal Growth and Change* (Washington, D.C.: Seven Locks Press, 1987).

Patrick R. Penland, *Self-Planned Learning in America* (Pittsburgh: Book Center, Graduate School of Library and Information Science, University of Pittsburgh, 1977).

Walter Perry, *The Open University: A Personal Account by the First Vice-Chancellor* (Milton Keynes, United Kingdom: Open University Press, 1976).

Michael Pilsworth and Ralph Ruddock, "Persons, Not Respondents: Alternative Approaches in the Study of Social Process," in *Creating Knowledge: A Monopoly*, ed. Budd Hall, Arthur Gillette, and Rajesh Tandon (New Delhi, India: Society for Participatory Research in Asia, 1982).

John Plamenatz, *Man and Society: a Critical Examination of Some Important Social and Political Theories from Machiavelli to Marx,* Volume 2 (London: Longmans, 1963).

Joan Robertson, Sharon Saberton, and Virginia Griffin, *Learning Partnerships: Interdependent Learning in Adult Education* (Toronto: Department of Adult Education, The Department of Adult Education, 1985).

Carl R. Rogers, *Client Centered Therapy: Its Current Practice, Implications, and Theory* (Boston: Houghton Mifflin, 1951).

Carl R. Rogers, *On Becoming a Person* (Boston: Houghton Mifflin, 1961).

Carl R. Rogers, *Freedom to Learn for the 80's* (Columbus, Ohio: Charles E. Merrill, 1983).

Dusan Savicevic, "Training Adult Educationists in Yugoslavia," *Convergence* 1: 1 (March, 1968).

David S. Stewart, *Adult Learning in America: Eduard Lindeman and His Agenda for Lifelong Education* (Malabar, Fla.: Kreiger, 1987).

Paul Tillich, *The Courage to Be* (New Haven: Yale University Press, 1952).

Allen Tough, *Why Adults Learn* (Toronto: The Ontario Institute for Studies in Education, 1967).

Allen Tough, *The Adult's Learning Projects: A Fresh Approach to Theory and Practice in Adult Learning*, 2nd ed. (Toronto: The Ontario Institute for Studies in Education, 1979).

Allen Tough, *Intentional Changes: A Fresh Approach to Helping People Change* (Chicago: Follett, 1982).

Allen Tough, Virginia Griffin, Bill Barnard, and Donald Brundage, *The Design of Self-Directed Learning*, ed. Reg. Herman (a package of print and videotaped materials) (Toronto: Department of Adult Education, the Ontario Institute for Studies in Education, and Ryerson Polytechnical Institute, 1980).

Ralph W. Tyler, *Basic Principles of Curriculum and Instruction* (Chicago: University of Chicago Press, 1949).

Linda J. Vogel, "Working with Older Adults," in *Handbook of Adult Religious Education*, ed. Nancy T. Foltz (Birmingham, Ala.: Religious Education Press, 1986).

H.J. Wallberg, D. Schiller, and G.D. Haertel, "The Quiet Revolution in Educational Research," *Kappan* 61 (1979).

Clay Warren, "Andragogy and N.F.S. Grundtwig: A Critical Link," *Adult Education Quarterly* 39: 4 (Summer, 1989).

John H. Westerhoff III, *Will Our Children Have Faith?* (New York: Seabury, 1976).

James W. White, *Intergenerational Religious Education: Models, Theory, and Prescription for Interage Life and Learning in the Faith Community* (Birmingham, Ala.: Religious Education Press, 1988).

Evelyn Whitehead and James Whitehead, *Christian Life Patterns: The Psychological Challenges and Religious Invitations of Adult Life* (New York: Doubleday, 1979).

R.E.Y. Wickett, "Adult Learning and Spiritual Growth," *Religious Education* 75: 5 (July-August, 1980).

R.E.Y. Wickett, "Working with Middle-Aged Adults," in *Handbook of Adult Religious Education*, ed. Nancy T. Foltz (Birmingham, Ala.: Religious Education Press, 1986).

R.E.Y. Wickett and Gregory Dunwoody, "The Religious Learning Projects of Catholic Adults in Early and Middle Adulthood," *Insight: A Journal of Adult Religious Education* 3 (1990).

H.A. Witkin, "The Nature and Importance of Individual Differences in Perception," *Journal of Personality* 18 (1949).

H.A. Witkin, "Individual Differences in Ease of Perception of Embedded Figures," *Journal of Personality* 19 (1950).

Blaine R. Worthen and James R. Sanders, *Educational Evaluation: Alternative Approaches and Practical Guidelines* (New York: Longman, 1987).

Index of Names

Index of Subjects

A number of subjects which the author believes will be of relevance to the reader are included in this list. Subjects which are found with great frequency in the volume will not have a complete listing. Only the most important references are included in this listing.

173